To my Dearest Jennette,

May you cont. leverage the power of Mentorship and reach your full Potential.

All the Best,
Adrienne M. Simek
9/23/23

MASTERING MENTORING TO YOUR VANTAGE POINT

ADRIENNE M. SOMERVILLE

Print ISBN: 979-8-21895-693-6
eBook ISBN: 9798-3-5090-928-9

ACKNOWLEDGEMENT

"Establishing a mentoring program within any organization provides learning and developmental opportunities for both team members and leaders. Informal relationships where knowledge and experiences are shared enables individual growth while building the organization's future leaders. Ms. Adrienne Somerville, who has spent her career developing others as a mentor and expert talent manager, now provides an excellent guide to master mentoring."

— Martin Ahmad
Department of the Navy Senior Executive Service Member (retired)
and Defense Industry Executive

FOR MANY YEARS, I HAVE RICHLY RECEIVED THE REWARDS resulting from various valuable types of mentoring. Today, I am committed to paying forward, all I have learned and mastered, to legacy leaders like you wanting to influence, shape and share your knowledge and information for the betterment of yourself and others whom you encounter.

One of my greatest takeaways is that mentorship has afforded me the opportunity to learn and approach mentoring with a holistic view. Specifically, in this book, you will gain insight into what I consider to be

"*the mentoring life cycle.*"

To all of my amazing mentors, please accept my heartfelt gratitude for your leadership and continued enduring support.

To all of my awesome mentees,

please accept this tribunal mentoring book because it offers

the ins and outs of how to guide yourself and others to success by leveraging mentorship.

DEDICATION

I WOULD LIKE TO FIRST THANK MY GRANDMOTHER, MS. CAROLYN E. Parker, for introducing me to the priceless power of mentorship. This book is truly a dedication and tribute to my remarkable grandmother's shared life-changing mentoring lessons.

Additionally, I would like to thank my family, friends and community members who shared their candid words of wisdom, in the spirit of mentoring me. Moreover, I would also like to humbly thank my amazing mentors, all who have shared their knowledge and experiences for my personal and professional betterment, covering more than half of a century.

Lastly, I would like to sincerely and wholeheartedly thank you for wanting to "level up" your mentoring game; to move beyond simply understanding the benefits of mentorship or the workings of a mentoring program, and purposefully embrace mentoring to your vantage point.

When reading *Mastering Mentoring to Your Vantage Point*, trust your instincts! It is my hope you remain intrigued, gain additional knowledge about mentorship, and become even more inspired to apply these highly regarded recommended best-in-class mentoring practices. All the BEST!

Cheering for you always,

Adrienne M. Somerville
Adrienne M. Somerville

TABLE OF CONTENTS

PREFACE: MY MENTORING JOURNEY 1

INTRODUCTION...5

CHAPTER 1: UNDERSTANDING MENTORING AND
ITS PURPOSE 9

CHAPTER 2: DO NOT CONFUSE MENTORING
WITH COACHING 19

CHAPTER 3: WHY IS MENTORING IMPORTANT? 25

CHAPTER 4:CRITICAL SKILLS FOR MENTORING
RELATIONSHIP SUCCESS: HOW DO YOU LEARN?
HOW DO YOU LISTEN? 31

CHAPTER 5: UNDERSTANDING THE MENTOR-
MENTEE RELATIONSHIP 53

CHAPTER 6: THE INITIAL MEETING...
AND THOSE THAT FOLLOW 77

CHAPTER 7: TRANSITIONING THE MENTOR-
MENTEE RELATIONSHIP 111

CONCLUSION 117

PREFACE:

MY MENTORING JOURNEY

I AM A STRONG BELIEVER AND BENEFACTOR OF EXEMPLARY mentorship. Hence, when writing my first book, *Wingspan: Talent Management Gaining Corporate Dominance*, I devoted an entire section to the topic, specifically Chapter 8, entitled "Discussing Mentorship and Its Organizational Value."

In today's overly complex and dynamic environment, it is ill-advised to navigate through any organization without developing and capitalizing on the value of mentorship. At times, I find it challenging to simply navigate through life without the insightful intellect and profound perspectives shared by my trusted mentors.

Throughout my entire life, I have been blessed to have amazing mentors. My very first mentor was my grandmother, Ms. Carolyn E. Parker. Long before I gained an appreciation and understanding of the value of mentorship, my grandmother exposed me to informal mentoring, by affording me the blessings of her knowledge, love and support. My grandmother's lessons still line the walls of my soul and echo in my spirit today, simply because her wisdom is timeless.

Upon graduating from college and entering the working world at the tender age of 22, I quickly realized success was not a solo adventure; it involved collaboration with others and leaving clues along the way, like a breadcrumb trail as a guide. Specifically, I watched leaders within my company not only mentor fellow workforce members, but capitalize on mentoring relationships with other leaders, both inside and outside of the organization. Additionally, I enjoyed witnessing how leveraging mentoring relationships were influencing and shaping the respective career trajectories of the mentees.

Interestingly, many of us spend time working extremely hard, investing in what I would call our "performance capital," while missing the opportunity to invest in our "relationship capital." Performance capital results from demonstrated commitment and hard work that yield outcomes contributing to organizational gains. Conversely, relationship capital results from meeting, connecting, and networking with people, as well as forming mentoring relationships with those people, which contribute to our individual goals. It has been my experience that personal and professional growth results from investing in both performance capital and relationship capital. Unfortunately, sometimes we simply ignore the relationship capital investment opportunities. And I'm here to tell you why *not* to do that.

Advancing throughout my career, I was continuously advised to identify, find and select a mentor. However, often missing was the "how" – especially early in my career. In particular, how to go about not just identifying a mentor, but selecting the best mentor for the unique chapter of my career and phase of my life. Today's hybrid work environment, and its reliance on digital platforms to invest in both performance capital and relationship capital, further exacerbates the challenge of many professionals identifying his or her optimal mentor.

The purpose of my book is to ensure you have the most thorough understanding of mentoring, and more importantly, how to directly access and have the strategic opportunities to meet with the mentors needed to influence and shape you and your career aspirations.

I am inspired by the continued conversations, symposiums, summits and workshops that surround the important topic of mentorship. Consequently, I felt the compelling necessity to author what will prove to be your invaluable mentoring workbook… a mentoring masterpiece, uniquely designed *for* you and customized *by* you.

INTRODUCTION

"A mentor is someone who allows you to see the hope within yourself."
— *Oprah Winfrey*

YOU ARE EXTREMELY SMART! YOU ARE HERE BECAUSE YOU want to thoroughly understand how to best approach mentoring, as well as how to fully embrace the power of mentorship. Among several thick books relating to mentoring, you chose this condense, non-traditional mentoring workbook to elevate your mentoring experience.

According to a recently published article in Forbes regarding a study on mentorships, 76 percent of people think mentors are important, however, only 37 percent of people currently have one. These numbers reflect quite a bit of disparity. Do you believe it is too challenging to secure a mentor, or are you unable to recognize and access potential mentors?

Mastering Mentoring to Your Vantage Point is the definitive book about mentoring. It was written to detail every aspect of mentorship, with an emphasis on the *how,* to establish and optimize your mentoring relationships so they exceed your aspirations and expectations, as well as enable you to achieve your personal and professional goals and objectives. *Mastering Mentoring to Your Vantage Point* imparts realistic insights and experiences on how to successfully navigate through mentoring relationships for your unique vantage point. As stated above, you are indeed extremely smart, and let us assume, audaciously ambitious. The supposition of your intrinsic motivation alone has led you to become familiar with how mentoring shall be your game-changer.

In Chapter 1, I define mentoring and the mentoring relationship, to include the role and responsibilities of both the mentor and mentee. Additionally, I will review of the various types of mentoring models. In Chapter 2, coaching is introduced because I want to ensure you understand both mentoring and coaching; their definitions, focus areas, approaches and needed skillsets, which are completely different yet complimentary. Chapter 3 answers why mentoring is so important to individuals and companies. It is important to understand the role you play as a mentor and mentee, and more importantly how mentoring impacts the individual, managers and organizations at large. Chapter 4 provides you the critical skills to ensure you have a successful mentoring relationship by teaching learning styles and effective listening tips. Frankly, mentoring should *always* be approached with a growth mindset. In Chapter 5, the attributes, characteristics and qualities of the best mentors and mentees are discussed to gift you with an expert level of understanding of how to cultivate a meaningful mentor and mentee relationship; one which includes selecting the right mentor for you. In Chapter 6, you learn more about the long-awaited topic of how to best initiate that first and second mentoring meeting, and all those needed discussions to follow, formulating a progressive mentoring relationship that is both meaningful and measurable. One thing is for certain, as you journey through your mentoring relationship, understanding how to transition the mentor-mentee relationship through preparation, agreements, relationship-building and closure is critical, so Chapter 7 is reserved for the pertinent mentoring life cycle discussion.

By now you are probably wondering, so what makes this book so special? Although there are many other books written on the topic of mentoring, the uniqueness of *Mastering Mentoring to Your Vantage Point*'s success depends solely on your level of engagement and willingness to do the mentoring work outlined in this book, with only you and your success in mind. This mentoring workbook includes inspiring quotes, guided self-assessments and self-discovery exercises, along with personal reflection activities, actionable worksheets for your documentation purposes, as well as questions and answers for your consideration and application. I know you are very busy and investing personal time to increase your understanding of mentorship. Therefore, for ease of learning and instead of providing hundreds of pages of unnecessary or redundant information, *Mastering Mentoring to Your Vantage Point* allows you to leverage the sample provided forms and checklist including the mentoring partnership agreement, mentoring partnership plan, goals for a mentor-mentee relationship, evaluation of mentee progress, and transitioning the mentoring relationship.

At the conclusion of this book, you will learn how to embark upon your mentoring journey competence, and how to "level up" in your mentoring relationship with confidence. The mentoring principles and processes shared will certainly enable you to extract the most from your mentoring relationships. As a result, I hope your takeaways lead to good insights and a strong impulse urging you to take immediate action to launch or leap along your mentoring journey.

CHAPTER 1:

UNDERSTANDING MENTORING
AND ITS PURPOSE

*"The mediocre mentor tells. The good mentor explains. The superior
mentor demonstrates. The greatest mentors inspire!"*
— Lucia Traynor

MENTORING EXPLAINED

MENTORING HAS A LONG HISTORY BEGINNING WITH THE
character Mentor in Homer's poem, "The Odyssey." This character was
the companion of Telemachus, Odysseus' son, providing guidance and
advice throughout the time he was away from his home and family.

A mentoring relationship consists of a mentor and a mentee. A
mentor is someone who influences, teaches, provides guidance or direction, or gives help and advice to a less experienced and often younger
person, the mentee. In a professional setting, a mentor helps you grow
your skills, make better decisions, and gain new perspectives on your

career. Rather than learning through trial and error, a mentor is a person you can talk to and gain a clear sense of direction.

Mentoring is a learning relationship where a mentor and mentee agree to a partnership, working collaboratively toward the achieving defined goals. The goals are usually discussed during the first meeting, focused on developing a mentee's skills, abilities, knowledge, and thinking. Goals can include attaining a specific skill, gaining exposure to a particular role or process, or testing ideas related to career progression or challenges within the organization.

Mentorships are powerful. Mentorships give people the support they need to reach higher levels. Mentors are valuable sources of information. A mentor can teach you about your organization and your industry or guide you and prevent you from making professional mistakes. A mentor is someone you can share ideas with and turn to for advice. Throughout a mentorship, you grow and progress professionally and learn to avoid common pitfalls.

Mentoring provides a safe place to learn, identify talents and explore career aspirations. Together with their mentor, mentees can focus on their long-term career, examine how and what to learn from their present job to be successful in future opportunities, or identify different career paths in general. They will learn how to enhance their visibility, develop their network, and become more open to move across organizational boundaries in both their daily work and future career ambitions.

"Mentoring is to support and encourage people to manage their own learning in order that they may maximize their potential, develop their skills, improve their performance and become the person they want to be."
— *Eric Parsloe*

Mentorship is a tool to help turn vision into reality. Mentors are expected to guide and advise, helping mentees achieve a successful career or overcome professional "skill gaps."

The purpose of mentoring is to create relationships where the existing knowledge, skills, and experience of senior or high-performing employees are shared and developed for newer or less experienced employees to advance their careers. Mentoring allows the mentee to take responsibility and accountability for their professional actions, behaviors, and solutions. It provides the opportunity for the mentee to identify and take ownership of their learning and development needs and is one of the best ways to accelerate your professional growth.

MENTORING MODELS

When you first think of mentoring, what comes to mind? You probably envision yourself sitting across from a senior leader participating in an in-depth conversation. The traditional and most often used mentoring form, the one-on-one model, is what comes to mind. However, mentoring has evolved to be able to address the broadest of potential opportunities for development and growth.

One-On-One Mentoring

This is the most popular model, one mentor and one mentee enter into a relationship to help the mentee develop, improve and achieve specific goals. The mentor is usually a senior member of the organization, in the same career field as the mentee. However, many mentees select a mentor outside their current field to provide insight, connections and knowledge outside their normal interactions. The mentor works closely with the mentee, and a long-term relationship is built and nurtured over time.

Many organizations offer a formal mentoring program where a process of "matching" the participants occurs. Employees actively research senior members, through a variety of methods, scheduling time to meet and "interview" each potential mentor. Regardless of method, once the mentor selection occurs, participants agree upon how often they will meet, length of meetings, and what goals the mentee wants to achieve. This mentoring model is focused on relationship-building and individual skill-building.

Peer Mentoring

Peer mentoring occurs when two people from a similar job level or age range commit to a mentoring relationship with the goal of sharing experiences, expertise, and learning together. In this style, each may take turns acting as mentor and mentee.

Peer mentoring works well as part of a targeted program, such as for onboarding new employees or providing support to employees changing career fields. For example, it has been successfully used in practicing for interviews or preparing to brief leadership. Peer mentoring also gives employees an opportunity to develop leadership and communication skills in a peer-to-peer environment.

Group Mentoring

There are occasions where the group mentoring model is also highly effective. As the name implies, there are numerous mentees participating with a single mentor. Group mentoring is used for situational mentoring scenarios. For example, when an organization is experiencing a significant change, wants to deliver a unified message, or inform on a singular topic. A select number of senior leaders will meet with a group of employees to inform, discuss, share, and address questions or concerns. The mentorship is usually of a shorter duration since there is a single objective. With group mentoring, the goal is for the members to gain understanding and clarity. The mentees are also able to meet with the mentors one-on-one if needed.

Group mentoring is able to reach and impact a larger number of mentees in a shorter amount of time than traditional mentoring. It is an effective way of "up-skilling" groups, sharing knowledge and fostering a culture of transparency. Additionally, this form of mentorship helps to improve every participant's teamwork.

Situational Mentoring

Occasions arise when you want employees to learn a new process, system or platform. It is highly effective to utilize situational mentoring, when a group is paired with an experienced employee to mentor until they get comfortable finding a mentor on their own. Situational mentoring is a blend of traditional one-on-one and group mentoring where a singular mentor develops the skills of a group, though it can also be available one-on-one as needed.

Similar to group mentoring, situational mentoring is of a shorter duration and has a singular goal; however, the participants may meet with greater frequency until the goal is achieved.

Reverse Mentoring

Reverse mentoring is when a more junior person mentors a more senior person in an organization. Essentially, this model represents the traditional one-on-one mentoring in reverse. Reverse mentoring recognizes there are skill gaps and learning opportunities on both sides of the organization. Examples where reverse mentoring is useful include "up-skilling" senior employees on digital technology or as part of a diversity and inclusion initiative. The reverse mentoring model can have one mentor and mentee or numerous mentees.

Speed (or Flash) Mentoring

Speed mentoring is useful for creating impactful knowledge sharing without the pressure to develop a long-term relationship. It is an effective and efficient way to introduce mentees to potential mentors and provide a setting to quickly demonstrate what a mentoring session is all about. A speed mentoring session offers a trial for a new mentoring relationship and helps individuals broaden exposure to senior leaders before committing to a longer-term mentorship.

Speed mentoring provides a timed session between potential mentees and mentors, with the mentees informed prior to the session to bring several questions for discussion. Even in a short amount of time, potential mentees quickly grasp the value a mentoring relationship can offer. Speed mentoring is often offered intermittently to allow employees to gain exposure to the experience.

Team Mentoring

Similar to sports, team mentoring involves a group of mentors and a group of mentees who participate in mentoring sessions as a team. The key difference between group mentoring and team mentoring is that team mentorship involves multiple mentors working with the group instead of just one.

Team mentoring is often used for a group working on a shared goal or project. Mentees have developmental goals they can work on together with the guidance of a number of mentors. This mentoring model can help promote diversity and inclusion, creating a space for numerous people with different opinions and perspectives to come together and learn.

As with group mentoring, this type of mentoring is good for teamwork and eliminates any potential of favoritism or elitism sometimes associated with one-on-one mentoring.

Virtual Mentoring

In response to remote work, which has become and remains vital in our modern working lives, virtual mentoring is an important and versatile mentoring model. Virtual mentoring expands mentorships exponentially, using a variety of apps and software for virtual communication. This opens mentoring relationships to include people in different cities and even globally.

Offering virtual mentoring opens opportunities for mentees to create mentorships with mentors outside their current location, which expands the ability to gain perspectives and exposure to senior leaders outside their zip code.

ESSENTIAL PRINCIPLES FOR THE MENTOR:

- Assess the mentee's skill, knowledge, and attitudes when offering advice.
- Allow the mentee to fail at times.
- Challenge the mentee.
- Be available when mentoring sessions are scheduled.
- Introduce the mentee to key contacts and possible collaborators.
- Pay attention to the mentee's development, goal achievements, and advancement.
- Tailor sessions to the individual mentee.
- Lead, but do not direct the mentee.
- Set high standards and articulate them clearly to the mentee.
- Provide constructive feedback in a timely manner.
- Be honest with your opinions and your perspective.
- Foster open communication and be an active listener.
- Discuss "survival skills."
- Collectively set goals and agenda for subsequent meetings.
- Inform the mentee of professional development opportunities.
- Assist the mentee with socio-political navigation.
- Assist the mentee with creating and prioritizing their career plan.
- Model professional behavior.
- View the mentee as a respected colleague.
- Do not seek to replicate yourself.
- Do not do the work for the mentee.

- Do not be offended if the mentee chooses not to take your advice.
- Do not become best friends with the mentee.

KEY ASPECTS OF MENTORING

Please note these are key shared aspects of every successful mentoring relationship.

Build Trust

Most importantly, trust must be developed between the mentor and mentee, especially if/when they work in the same organization. To develop trust, a series of ground rules must be established and adhered to, allowing each participant to feel comfortable.

The ground rules should include maintaining scheduled meetings, determining the mentee's preference for receiving candid feedback, the confidentiality of all discussions, etc. The trust developed between the mentor and mentee allows each to be free to share honest insights and grow the relationship.

Establish Goals and Share Lessons Learned

To ensure you quickly begin focusing on the goals the mentee wants to achieve, the mentor must create an environment where discussion is comfortable. It is the mentor's responsibility to initiate the discussion that allows the mentee to identify what they want to achieve.

The most common goals mentees identify include the desire to improve presentation and public speaking skills, develop executive presence, enhance networking skills, as well as overall career development. In many cases, the mentee may not know how to articulate the goals they want to achieve. When that occurs, usually during the initial meeting, the mentor must invest the time to ask questions intended to help the mentee determine what's important to achieve, listen and offer suggestions.

Mentors should share their path, the ups and downs and how they responded, what they learned, and how they've applied those lessons over their career and life. This includes sharing the "tough love" lessons learned, which means being willing to be completely honest. It is important for the mentor to be confident enough to share the situations that did not go well, or ones in which they wish they had acted differently. The sharing of the highs and lows, as a mentor, will assist the mentee with understanding that no one ascends to senior leadership positions or where they want to be without course correcting their behaviors, at times. Please note the word *failure* was purposefully not used.

Take Action

The traditional one-on-one mentoring meetings usually occur quarterly and last an hour. While the initial meeting may feel informal and like a discussion, subsequent meetings will have a distinct objective: moving the mentee closer to goal achievement. Mentors need to be prepared to have an agenda in place to keep the meeting on track and moving forward. It is important to always remember that mentoring is action oriented. The mentee's goals will not be achieved without a plan and deliberate, continued effort focused on outcomes.

Most meetings will begin with an agenda that includes discussing progress that has been made since the last meeting. If progress has not occurred, a discussion of what challenges has impeded progress. Be prepared for occasions where an issue or conflict has occurred, and the mentee wants to invest the allotted hour venting and looking for advice.

Throughout the mentorship, it is common for the relationship between the mentor and mentee to grow. As a result, the first several minutes of the conversation will likely evolve into more of a "catch up", than an overview of what is going to be accomplished.

"Catch up" conversations are perfectly normal and encouraged because they demonstrate how comfortable the two of you have become, trust that has gown, and the willingness to openly share progress or challenges.

Celebrate Successes

Celebrating success is incredibly important. Celebrating milestones, achievements, large and small, is key to showing progress. It is significant for several reasons. Yes, it demonstrates the mentee has made progress and either achieved a goal or made strides toward achieving their goal. But more importantly, investing the time to recognize success, demonstrates that you, their mentor, is paying attention and sincerely invested.

The mentor's approval is important, and the mentor of all people, know the efforts they have expended to arrive at this point. Celebrating success is also a moment for the mentor to congratulate themselves for the positive impact their efforts have made toward their mentee's goals or achievement.

CHAPTER 2:

DO NOT CONFUSE MENTORING WITH COACHING

"A coach has some great questions for your answers;
a mentor has some great answers for your questions."
— Unknown

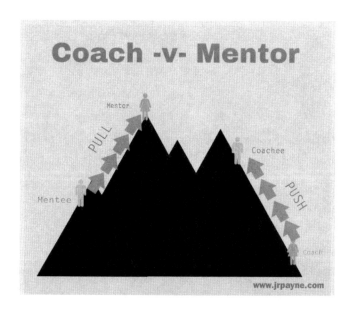

UNDERSTANDING MENTORING AND COACHING

FREQUENTLY PEOPLE USE THE WORDS "MENTORING" AND "coaching" interchangeably, but they are not the same type of relationship. Both share specific goals that work toward employee learning and career development. However, the definition, focus, role, approach, and tools of each are different. An organization is not required to choose between mentoring or coaching relationships and programs. Each improves the participant's ability to contribute to the organization's goals.

Chapter 1 defined mentoring. The International Coaching Federation (ICF), however, defines coaching as, "a partnering with clients in a thought-provoking and creative process that inspires them to maximize their personal and professional potential. The process of coaching often unlocks previously untapped sources of imagination, productivity and leadership."

ROLES AND DURATION

MENTORING: The mentor talks *with* a person who has identified their needs prior to entering into a mentoring relationship. The focus is on active listening, providing information, making suggestions, and establishing connections. Mentoring is often long-term with some relationships lasting years or even decades. In fact, some famous mentors and mentees cite lifelong mentoring relationships.

COACHING: The coach listens *to* a person, identifies what they need, and helps them develop an action plan. The emphasis is on the person finding the solution, not instructing or leading them. Coaching is often short-term and may be as short as a quick 10 or 15-minute conversation.

APPROACH

MENTORING: The mentoring relationship is developed between the mentor and mentee. Mentorship is most frequently initiated by a mentee selecting a mentor, with the two discussing and deciding upon the goals, ground rules and a course of action. Mentoring is more directive, with the mentor sharing their knowledge, experience and skills. The Mentor guides and advises the mentee to achieve their goals. Mentoring focuses on development and expects the mentee to decide which goals they have for their mentoring relationships.

COACHING: The coaching relationship is more structured. The participants are working within a narrow perspective; their agenda is specific, the relationship is for a short period of time, and the goal focuses on certain results. Coaching is non-directive; it focuses on asking the right questions, providing the space, trust and confidence for the individual to determine how they can achieve more, reach their objectives and find capabilities within themselves. Coaching is performance-driven and encourages the individual or individuals being coached to perform in their day-to-day roles.

TOOLS AND TRAINING

MENTORING: The most important tool is the mentoring agreement, which is developed, completed, and signed by the mentor and mentee. This document formalizes commitment to the mentoring relationship and includes the mentee's goals, meeting schedule and preferred communication methods. No formal qualifications are required for mentoring. Mentor training is often recommended, but the organization rarely creates, or imposes standard criteria.

COACHING: A coaching agreement sets the ground rules for the partnership. Many organizations use the 360-degree or skills assessments in preparation for the coaching sessions. The majority of coaches have certifications based on structured training and qualifications.

SKILLS REQUIRED FOR MENTORING

- Experience, knowledge, and insights in the area in which you're providing mentoring. Mentoring is built on solid advice and guidance.
- Relationship-building and interpersonal skills are crucial for mentoring.
- Motivating, encouraging, and inspiring energy throughout all mentoring meetings
- Active listening skills are essential.
- The ability to ask open-ended questions when helping the mentee identify their goals.

SKILLS REQUIRED FOR COACHING

- The ability to maximize resources and inspire.
- The ability to recognize the strengths and challenges of the individual being coached in order to propel them forward.
- The ability to address problems directly and not allow the individual being coached to dwell on them.
- The ability to raises awareness and responsibility both with the individual being coached but also throughout an overall office or entire organization.
- The ability to find the right balance of interpersonal skills and the practical skills to convert discussions into actions.

The reason coaching and mentoring are so frequently used interchangeably is due to the number of comparable characteristics:

- Defined roles allow participants to envision the achievement of desired goals.
- Both relationships require trust, respect, open communication, and flexibility.
- Participants can include any member of the organization: new hires, new managers, and staff promoted to senior level positions.
- Success is achieved when senior leaders understand the return on investment and organizational goals regarding engagement, performance, and retention are achieved.

The objective is to achieve both individual and organization goals.

Differences between Mentoring and Coaching

	Mentoring	Coaching
Focus:	Individual Development	Performance Improvement
Role:	no agenda	Specific agenda
Relationship:	Self-selecting	Comes with the position
Source of Influence:	Perceived value	Position
Arena:	Life / Career	Business or sports
Time Frame:	Long term	Short term
Agenda:	Open	Set
Orientation:	relationship related	Task related
Approach:	Non-structured	structured
Personal Objective:	Improved performance	Personal satisfaction

Thepeakperformancecenter.com

CHAPTER 3:

WHY IS MENTORING IMPORTANT?

"Mentoring isn't an extracurricular activity.
It is vital for cultivating an enriching, inclusive community."
— Diana Olin

IMPORTANCE OF MENTORING: TO INDIVIDUALS

IT MAY SEEM IRONIC TO SHARE, BUT THE FOUNDATION OF A successful mentoring relationship is choosing a mentor who has a deep understanding and experience in how your business works. A mentor provides:

Advice

One of the significant, if not priceless, benefits of the mentor-mentee relationship is advice from a senior person with more experience. Mentors provide answers to questions, make suggestions, share their network, and assist in navigating your career progression within the organization.

Perspective

Mentors also share context and perspectives often not previously considered. For example, their experience provides knowledge about similar challenges and situations that can help you avoid common professional missteps. Additionally, a mentor's experience can provide a differing perspective, relate diverse leadership experiences, and ask a different set of questions.

Improving Skills

Mentors are invested in helping mentees develop business skills and achieve professional goals. Most mentorships are for the long term.

Networking

Networking is vital for climbing the corporate ladder and mentors have valuable connections throughout the organization. Mentors open their network to the mentee, which result in numerous benefits.

Methods and Strategies

Mentors are a source of proven strategies to prevent or address problems when they arise.

Long-lasting Relationships

One of the most significant benefits of mentorship is the chance to collaborate throughout the course of your careers

Confidence and Encouragement

Sometimes all it takes to make important business decisions is confidence. Mentors are perfectly positioned to provide guidance and reinforce their mentee's business skills, making them more self-assured in their interactions.

Improved Career Outcomes

Studies have confirmed mentored employees receive a greater number of promotions and higher compensations as mentees become visible to leadership across the organization. Through mentoring, there is a higher likelihood that mentees will seek promotions as they become aware of potential opportunities.

Satisfaction and Career Commitment

Mentoring affords an opportunity to discuss the job, its challenges, and career options with a diverse group of managers and leaders throughout the organization. Specifically, mentors also provide the ability to link the mentee's contributions to the overall success of the organization.

Effects on Leadership

Good mentors help new professionals learn skills beyond what is taught in professional training, such as management principles and leadership best practices. Perlman, a leader within the Forbes organization, sums this concept up very well when he states, "The value of a mentor who can help cultivate leadership skills one-on-one in real-time, reduce the anxiety in taking big steps, and focus leaders on achieving their goals — is huge."

IMPORTANCE OF MENTORING: TO COMPANIES

The most valuable resources in an organization are the employees. Mentoring, whether through an established program or decided between individuals, strategically develops talent, and helps ensure they contribute to the growth, innovation, and bottom line of the organization.

Studies show Millennials are becoming the dominant force in the workplace, which makes mentoring more important than ever before. Employees, especially the younger generations, are less loyal to their organizations and this impacts retention. Investing in mentoring impacts the capability, performance, and success of the organization both short-term and long-term. Mentoring benefits organizations by:

Increasing Employee Engagement

Mentoring programs increase employee engagement due to their structure and approach. Mentoring is designed for employees, and it addresses their issues, challenges, and weaknesses. Mentoring increases employee interest at work. Mentees tend to not lose interest because they realize the benefit of having a mentor to guide them on how to achieve professional goals and deal with various career challenges.

Employee Engagement Powers Revenue, Sales and Customer Satisfaction

A company's revenue and sales increase when employees are more engaged, and mentored employees are proven to be more engaged. Engaged employees work hard to sell products and services and have the confidence to try new approaches with customers.

Mentoring Programs Result in an Increase in Productivity

Productivity depends on several factors. Specifically, the mindset and skillset of employees. Mentoring is an established way to ensure employees develop a suitable skill set and attitude. A company's productivity increases as the employee mindset develops to show increased performance and the ability to overcome weaknesses.

Millennials Want a Mentor

Millennials are different from previous generations in many ways. One difference is that millennials want someone continuously guiding them on how to do things. The desire to have a mentor is an opportunity for companies to train employees for high productivity and address or resolve problems through guidance and advice of the mentor. Mentoring certainly ensures millennial employees stay focused.

Mentoring Programs Result in Higher Retention, Lower Turnover Rates

High turnover rates and low retention rates are not suitable for any company. One of the many reasons companies invest in mentoring programs is to lower their turnover rates and increase employee retention. The accumulated effect of improved career outcomes, increased satisfaction and career commitment reduces intentions to leave, causing the actual turnover among mentored employees to decline.

Top Talents Are Attracted to Companies with Mentoring Programs

Talented people have more professional options, and often purposefully choose to work for an organization where they can grow and flourish over time. Mentoring programs are an excellent attraction for top talent because they realize mentoring empowers them with new skills and knowledge.

CHAPTER 4:

CRITICAL SKILLS FOR MENTORING RELATIONSHIP SUCCESS: HOW DO YOU LEARN? HOW DO YOU LISTEN?

"When you talk, you are only repeating what you already know. But if you listen, you may learn something new."
– Dalai Lama

LEARNING STYLES

THE TERM LEARNING STYLES REFERS TO THE CONCEPT THAT there are different methods of learning or understanding new information; the way a person takes in, understands, expresses, and remembers information. According to the VAK (Visual, Auditory, Kinetic) learning styles, there are four primary learning styles: visual, auditory, kinesthetic and reading/writing. When delving into the study of learning styles, some incorporate as many as seven distinct styles, adding logical, social, and solitary; however, those additional three are not commonly agreed upon.

Not all people fit neatly into one of the four categories, but each type of learner exhibits specific traits found within the styles. People commonly have a main preferred learning style, yet still use a blend of all four. When you know your preferred learning style(s), you can better understand the type of learning that best suits you.

Why are learning styles a topic for mentoring? Both the mentor and mentee will be working toward achieving specific goals, and very frequently, those goals include learning a new skill. Knowing how the mentee learns guides manneer in which the new material should be presented.

VISUAL LEARNERS: LEARN MORE THROUGH VISUAL OR SPATIAL REPRESENTATIONS

How to Recognize Visual Learners:

Someone with a visual learning style prefers to take in information through pictures, diagrams, demonstrations, displays, handouts, films, flipchart, and more. They are partial to seeing and observing things, including graphic designs, charts, written directions, images, and anything that illustrates ideas. This is also referred to as the spatial learning style.

Individuals who learn through sight understand information better when it is presented in a visual way. These are ones who doodle, make lists, and take notes. Employees with visual-spatial intelligence can recall knowledge and details when pictured in their heads. Similarly, visual learners retain information better when they visualize the connections between data as they process the new information. These people will use phrases such as, "show me," or, "let's have a look at that," and be best able to perform a new task after reading the instructions or watching someone else do it first. These are the people who will work from lists and written directions and instructions.

How to Cater to Visual Learners:

In this instance, a whiteboard or smartboard can provide maximum effectiveness. Give them opportunities to write notes or directions. Use handouts and presentations. Visual learners may also need more time to process material, as they observe the visual cues, so allow them a little time and space to absorb the information.

Gamified lessons are best used for this type of learning, since there is a use of game-like elements that are big on interactive and visually appealing. Some gamification templates use include memory, image/word match, and more.

AUDITORY LEARNERS: LEARN MORE WHEN THE SUBJECT MATTER IS REINFORCED BY SOUND

How to Recognize Auditory Learners:

Someone with an auditory learning style prefers the transfer of information through listening to the spoken word or sounds and noises. These people will use phrases such as, "tell me," or, "let's talk it over," and will be best able to perform a new task after listening to instructions from an expert.

These learners are happy being given spoken instructions over the telephone and can remember all the words to songs they hear. These individuals would much rather listen to new information or a lecture than read written notes, often use their own voices to reinforce new concepts and ideas, as well as prefer reading out loud to themselves. They are not afraid to speak in public and are great at verbally explaining things. Additionally, they may be slower at reading and often repeat things told to them. This type of learning is also called aural learning and employees who fall under this category process the course lessons when presented to them vocally. Some examples of this type of learning style include music, lectures, podcasts, and talks. Auditory learners prefer vocal collaboration and communication where they read out loud lessons to absorb the information in their head.

How to Cater to Auditory Learners:

Auditory learners do well in the lecture by asking them to repeat new concepts back to you. Ask questions and let them answer. Invoke group discussions so your auditory and verbal processors can properly take in and understand the information they are presented. Watching videos and using music or audiotapes are also helpful ways of learning for this group.

KINESTHETIC LEARNERS: LEARN MORE THROUGH EXPERIENCING OR DOING

How to Recognize Kinesthetic Learners:

Someone with a kinesthetic learning style prefers learning from physical experience – touching, feeling, holding, doing, and practical hands-on exercises. These people will use phrases such as, "let me try," or, "how do you feel?" and will be best able to perform a new task by going ahead and trying it out, learning as they go. These are the people who like to experiment and never look at the instructions first. This group prefers to get involved by acting out events or using their hands to touch and handle items in order to understand concepts. They use the different senses to absorb information. This style of learning is also known as tactile or experiential learning. This is best used in fields that require interactive lessons to better explain the topic at hand. By involving the learners in the process of creating, planning, and solving, they absorb the lessons more by experiencing them firsthand. Some examples of kinesthetic learning include laboratory sessions, immersions or simulations, and hands-on workshops.

How to Cater to Kinesthetic Learners:

Kinesthetic learners do well by getting them moving. Incorporate movement into lessons such as pacing to help memorize, learning activities that involve moving around, or writing on a whiteboard. Once kinesthetic learners can physically sense what they are studying, abstract ideas and difficult concepts become easier to understand.

READING/WRITING LEARNERS: LEARN THROUGH WRITTEN WORDS

How to Recognize Reading/Writing Learners:

Someone with a reading/writing learning style learn through just that… reading and writing. This style of learning is drawn to expression through reading articles or books, writing notes or in diaries, researching, and searching the internet. Additionally, these learners tend to use tools and approaches, such as glossaries, re-reading notes and textbooks, re-writing their notes out in different relatable and relevant words, lists, and/or the simple rearrangement of information. Also, word choice matters deeply to reading/writing learners. Hence, sometimes these learners keep running glossaries of new words or unfamiliar terms for future reference.

How to Cater to Reading/Writing Learners:

Of the four learning styles, this is the easiest to cater to since much of the traditional educational system tends to center on writing essays, doing research, and reading books. Be mindful about allowing plenty of time for these individuals to absorb information through the written word and give them opportunities to share their ideas .

EXERCISE: LEARNING STYLES ACTIVITY

For each question, select the answer that most represents how you generally behave.

It is best to complete the questionnaire before reading the accompanying explanation.

1. When I operate new equipment, I generally:
   a) read the instructions first
   b) listen to an explanation from someone who has used it before
   c) go ahead and start, I can figure it out as I use it

2. When I need directions for travelling, I usually:
   a) look at a map
   b) ask for spoken directions
   c) follow my nose and maybe use a compass

3. When I cook a new dish, I like to:
   a) follow a written recipe
   b) call a friend for an explanation
   c) follow my instincts, testing as I cook

4. If I am teaching someone something new, I tend to:
   a) write instructions down
   b) give them a verbal explanation
   c) demonstrate first and then let them try it

5. I tend to say:
   a) watch how I do it
   b) listen to me explain
   c) go ahead

6. During my free time, I most enjoy:
   a) going to museums and galleries
   b) listening to music and talking to my friends
   c) playing sports or do-it-yourself (DIY)

7. When I go shopping for clothes, I tend to:
   a) imagine what they would look like on
   b) discuss them with the shop staff
   c) try them on and test them

8. When I am choosing a vacation, I usually:
   a) read lots of brochures
   b) listen to recommendations from friends
   c) imagine what it would be like to be there

9. If I was buying a new car, I would:
   a) read reviews in newspapers and magazines
   b) discuss what I need with my friends
   c) test-drive lots of different types

10. When I am learning a new skill, I am most comfortable:
    a) watching what the instructor is doing
    b) talking through exactly what I'm supposed to do
    c) giving it a try myself and work it out as I go

11. If I am choosing food off a menu, I tend to:
    a) imagine what the food will look like
    b) talk through the options in my head or with my partner
    c) imagine what the food will taste like

12. When I listen to a band, I can't help:
    a) watching the band members and other people in the audience
    b) listening to the lyrics and the beats
    c) moving in time with the music

13. When I concentrate, I most often:
    a) focus on the words or the pictures in front of me
    b) discuss the problem and the possible solutions in my head
    c) move around a lot, fiddle with pens and pencils and touch things

14. I choose household furnishings because I like:
    a) their colors and how they look
    b) the descriptions the salespeople give me
    c) their textures and what they feel like

15. My first memory is of:
    a) looking at something
    b) being spoken to
    c) doing something

16. When I am anxious, I:
    a) visualize the worst-case scenarios
    b) talk over in my head what worries me most
    c) can't sit still, fiddle and move around constantly

17. I feel especially connected to other people because of:
    a) how they look
    b) what they say to me
    c) how they make me feel

18. When I have to study, I generally:
    a) write lots of revision notes and diagrams
    b) talk over my notes, alone or with other people
    c) imagine making the movement or creating the formula

19. If I am explaining how to do something to someone, I tend to:
    a) show them what I mean
    b) explain to them in different ways until they understand
    c) encourage them to try it on their own and then talk them through my idea as they do it

20. I really love:
    a) watching films, photography, looking at art or people watching
    b) listening to music, the radio or talking to friends
    c) taking part in sporting activities, eating fine foods and wines or dancing

21. Most of my free time is spent:
    a) watching television
    b) talking to friends
    c) doing physical activity or making things

22. When I first contact a new person, I usually:
    a) arrange a face-to-face meeting
    b) talk to them on the telephone
    c) try to get together while doing something else, such as an activity or a meal

23. I first notice how people:
    a) look and dress
    b) sound and speak
    c) stand and move

24. If I am angry, I tend to:
    a) keep replaying in my mind what it is that has upset me
    b) raise my voice and tell people how I feel
    c) stamp about, slam doors and physically demonstrate my anger

25. I find it easiest to remember:
    a) faces
    b) names
    c) things I have done

26. I think you can tell if someone is lying if:
    a) they avoid looking at you
    b) their voices change
    c) they give me funny vibes

27. When I meet an old friend:
    a) I say, "It is great to see you!"
    b) I say, "It is great to hear from you!"
    c) I give them a hug or a handshake

28. I remember things best by:
    a) writing notes or keeping printed details
    b) saying them aloud or repeating words and key points in my head
    c) doing and practicing the activity or imagining it being done

29. If I have to complain about faulty goods, I am most comfortable:
    a) writing a letter
    b) complaining over the phone
    c) taking the item back to the store or posting it to head office

30. I tend to say:
    a) I see what you mean
    b) I hear what you are saying
    c) I know how you feel

Now add up how many A's, B's and C's you selected.

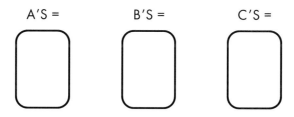

A'S =   B'S =   C'S =

If you chose mostly A, you have a VISUAL learning style.

If you chose mostly B, you have an AUDITORY learning style.

If you chose mostly C, you have a KINESTHETIC learning style.

Some people find their learning style may be a blend of two or three of the main learning styles: visual, auditory, kinesthetic, which excludes the reading/writing learning style. In this case, read about the styles that apply to you in the explanation earlier in the workbook. When you have identified your visual, auditory or kinesthetic learning style(s), read the learning styles explanations and consider how this might help you to identify learning and development that best meets your preference(s).

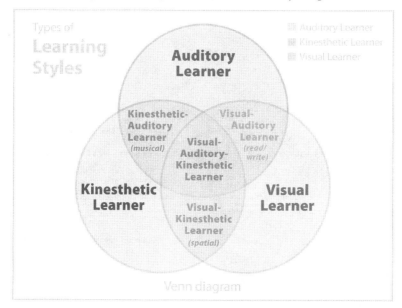

educationcorner.com/learning-styles

APPEALING TO THE DIFFERENT LEARNING STYLES AS A MENTOR

Visual Learners

To ensure that you have provided the needed stimulus for the visual mentee, create training programs that offer visual stimuli. Include brightly colored papers, markers, and posters with content that ties to the session topic and previous concepts that learners have experienced. This allows mental images to connect and provides reinforcement of key program elements.

Offer quotes, stories, analogies, and examples that are relative to points made in the session and provide mental images for learners. Use cartoons, graphics, and caricatures on handouts, flip charts, and other visual aids. If you use multimedia presentations, include animation and color. Add video segments that will supplement program content and discussions. Also include visualization activities where the mentee is asked to envision how certain situations would appear if they applied content discussed in the session. Visual learners represent 65 percent of the three learning styles.

Auditory Learners

To help meet the needs of your auditory learning mentees, prepare sessions that include opportunities for verbal exchanges. Incorporate a variety of stimulation, discussion, music, debates, role plays, audio involving verbal explanations. Auditory learners represent 30 percent of the three learning styles.

Kinesthetic Learners

To help ensure you have addressed the needs of the kinesthetic mentee, design programs and activities in which movement is a regular part of the learning. Move to other locations at various points for discussions, or use demonstrations, simulations, stretching, or energizers. Encourage role playing, in-basket (a training method that tests an individual's adaptive, thinking, judgment, problem-solving skills, planning, and organizational skills, decision-making, and prioritization), or other similar activities where learners have to handle things, interact, or move. Have actual items available for touching or exploration when possible. When actual items are not available, try to use mockups (models that look like the real object), simulators or other substitutes. Kinesthetic learners represent 5 percent of the three learning styles.

Reading/Writing Learners

Although there are three main learning styles, some individuals recognize another type that is very close to the main three, the fourth being the reading/writing learner. To help meet the needs of reading/writing learning mentees, it is important to leverage various types of reference materials because they prefer to learn by reading and writing notes, handouts, textbooks, and workbooks, such as this one. These types of mentees prefer to read and reread notes silently, over and over and over again.

WHY LISTENING IS ESSENTIAL TO SUCCESSFUL MENTORING

There is a famous saying, "One who listens need not say much." Listening is essential to a good mentor who must understand, translate, evaluate, and react to what a mentee is saying. Listening well takes practice and patience. It is an important skill but unlike talking, reading and writing, listening is not taught.

Mentors and mentees benefit from listening to share knowledge and challenges as they worked toward achieving the mentees goals. There is a key difference between listening and hearing. Hearing is a passive response and listening is an active action. Although we spend a lot of time hearing, experts estimate that only 25-50 percent of this time is spent actually listening.

Active listening is a simple technique which, when used with effective questioning, allows for more efficient and clear understanding, and increasing the chances of achieving positive outcomes. Active listening is consciously listening for cues and clues of the actual meaning in a message. Active listening includes not making assumptions or attempting to arrive at an answer, because our experiences lead us to believe we already know what is going to be said.

Why is Listening Essential?

When mentors actively listen to their mentees, it increases their ability to understand the conversation's underlying emotions. Actively listening to gain full understanding helps mentors prepare to accomplish goals. When the mentor says phrases such as, "I believe you are trying to increase your motivation," "You sound very discouraged," or, "We need to determine how to find a better balance between work and life," it helps the mentee gain confidence that the mentors understand their feelings.

Listening Skills Can Be Improved: Setting the Stage

Listening is a skill and like any other skill, it takes practice to improve. Luckily, since listening occurs throughout our daily lives, numerous opportunities present themselves to consciously try different techniques and monitor improvement. To increase listening abilities:

1. CREATE A NO-DIVERSION ATMOSPHERE

Mentors must listen to mentees in the same manner they would like to be listened to. Mentors can assist with their focus by creating an atmosphere with no diversion, undivided attention, and honest conversation. The more a mentor is open to hearing, the more a mentee will be comfortable in sharing.

The mentee must also work to remain diversion-free. Concentrating on the mentor while "shutting off" outside thoughts takes practice and discipline. Turning off cell phones, not permitting disruptions throughout the meeting, and presenting material in the mentee's preferred learning style are all practical and effective actions.

2. USE GROUND RULES IN PROGRAM SESSIONS

When mentors are active listeners, mentees are encouraged to talk during the sessions. Earlier the recommendation for establishing ground rules was shared. It is advised to include expected conduct for mentoring sessions. The list could include punctual arrival, no interrupting the speaker, no profanity, etc. Developing the parameters to ensure a comfortable and efficient session during the initial meeting will pay great dividends in the future.

3. ASK QUESTIONS USING THE RIGHT WORDS

Communication is key to successful mentoring. Mentors often struggle to completely understand the mentee's challenge, issue, or goal. In those situations, open-ended questions are helpful of getting to the crux. When constructing questions, mentors need to stay focused, clear, and remain on topic. They should consciously select words directed toward gaining helpful answers. Mentoring relationships are sensitive and evolving, so it is essential to maintain clear communication to avoid incorrect judgments and assumptions.

Mentees also need to try to find the best word to accurately portray their feelings or issue. When struggling, especially early in the mentoring relationship, the mentee is encouraged to say, "I'm struggling to find the right word. I'm thinking X, Y, and Z, but those do not accurately describe what I'm trying to say." This allows the mentor to try to ask a few questions to assist with reaching understanding.

4. MAINTAIN AN UNBIASED APPROACH

Every person has biases; however, every person is not fully aware of their biases. A good mentor recognizes they are listening to one side of a situation and must listen without judgement. This is one of the reasons seasoned individuals are chosen as mentors. In the majority of situations, mentors can envision the situation at a macro level to help guide the mentee's upcoming actions.

Mentees also bring bias to the mentoring session. Occasionally, the mentor will help the mentee recognize a bias was at the foundation of the situation or the interpretation of someone else's remarks. Mentees must be ready to accept different perspectives and receive honest input.

5. REMEMBER LISTENING IS ONLY PART OF THE EQUATION

Being conscious of the approach to questioning is important, but if the mentor or mentee do not listen to what they are told, the effectiveness of the word choices and questions is irrelevant and the opportunity to demonstrate interest and understanding was missed.

Mentors need to recognize the importance of sending cues of attentiveness. Physical actions to clearly demonstrate attention to the speaker, include leaning in, making eye contact, and folding hands. Additionally, while allowing the mentee to speak, the mentor can also use affirmations such as nodding, smiling or saying "yes" as other signs of attention and interest. Each of these represents significant signals to mentees that their mentor is interested and engaged.

BARRIERS TO EFFECTIVE LISTENING

Everyone has difficulty staying completely focused during a lengthy presentation or conversation, and sometimes, even relatively brief messages. Some of the factors that interfere with listening exist outside our control, but many are manageable. It is important to be aware of the prominent barriers to minimize their disruption.

Noise

Noise is one of the biggest factors to interfere with listening. Noise is anything that interferes with your ability to focus on and understand a message. There are many types of noise. The four you are most likely to encounter are: physical noise, psychological noise, physiological noise, and semantic noise.

- **Physical noise** is any sort of outside communication by someone or something. For example, a loud noise that interrupts or distracts you.
- **Psychological noise** are the distractions to a speaker's message caused by a receiver's internal thoughts. For example, if you are preoccupied with personal problems, it is difficult to give your full attention to understanding the message.
- **Psychological noise** is an ongoing mental conversation that never stops. This is an internal conversation or internal monologue that happens in the mind. Examples include: If someone's stomach is growling, this can distract them in the middle of a conversation, causing them to stop speaking and forget what they were going to say next, or if someone has a migraine causing light sensitivity, they may be unable to read notes on the board.
- **Semantic noise** is the interference during the construction of a message, such as when there are unfamiliar words.

Attention Span

A person can only maintain focused attention for a finite amount of time. Many people believe modern individuals have lost the ability to sustain attention to a message. It could be attributed to the competing messages and constant ability to connect. Few could predict how the cell phone and internet could impact the population's attention span. Think of the number of times (and places) you stop to check your phone or interrupt a conversation to receive a call.

Receiver Biases

As shared earlier, listening involves keeping an open mind and withholding judgment until the speaker has completed the message. Conversely, biased listening is characterized by ending the listening process and allowing your thoughts to jump to conclusions. The biased listener believes, "I do not need to listen because I already know this." Receiver biases are in reference to the speaker or preconceived ideas and opinions about the topic or message.

Listening Apprehension

This concept represents the fear that you might be unable to understand the message, process the information correctly, or be able to adapt your thinking to logically include the new information. Listening apprehension includes situations where you worry the information presented will be too complex for you to understand the full meaning.

THE EARS LISTENING MODEL

Empathize
- **Understand speaker's perspective**

Acknowledge
- **Use responsive communication**

Reflect
- **Repeat key words and pause to think**

Summarize
Frequently summarize what has been said

After preparing to active listen, and minimize any barriers in your control, the following active listening technique provides specific activities to improve your current listening skill level. These guidelines are from *"Clean Language"* by Wendy Sullivan and Judy Rees.

1. Put your attention on what the other person is actually saying rather than on the person themselves or what you think they might mean by their words.
2. Soft focus your eyes to take in the whole scene, rather than looking into the eyes of the other person.
3. Give them time: do not be impatient for your chance to talk.
4. Set your personal agenda aside, at least temporarily.
5. Visualize: mentally create your own model or diagram of what the other person is saying, but remember it is just that – *your* diagram or model, not theirs.
6. Believe what the other person is saying. Treat the words as if they are literally true, because for the speaker, they probably are.
7. Repeat back some of their words or phrases exactly as you heard them.
8. Take notes, if appropriate and it helps you pay attention.
9. Know your best listening state.
10. Turn your internal commentator down or off.
11. Be curious.
12. Practice!

ALSO:

1. Be calm – the calmer you are, the more attentively you will listen and the more you will encourage the other person to talk openly.

2. Adopt a posture that indicates to the other person you are listening. This will also send a signal to yourself that you are in listening mode.

3. Slowly tune out the rest of the world to focus on the other person.

4. Suspend judgement – take an attitude of listening to understand rather than assess. Try to avoid drawing conclusions either about the person or the issue.

5. Listen with your eyes and intuition as well as your ears: look for dissonance between what is said and what other senses tell you.

6. Listen to the emotion and mood of what is said, as well as the content.

7. Let go of the need to speak and to make your own points, until you have listened to all there is to hear.

8. Listen for what is *not said.*

9. Listen for patterns and themes – in the words people use, the images they evoke, the emotions they reveal.

10. Do not feel obliged to keep asking questions: less is more.

11. Allow space for silence; do not feel obliged to fill the space.

PERSONAL REFLECTION:

Reflect on your listening skills.

I listen most easily when:

_____

_____

_____

_____

_____

_____

_____

I have difficulty listening when:

_____

_____

_____

_____

_____

_____

_____

I am most attentive when:

_____

_____

_____

_____

_____

_____

_____

I am least attentive when:

_____

_____

_____

_____

_____

_____

_____

CHAPTER 5:

UNDERSTANDING THE MENTOR-MENTEE RELATIONSHIP

"Colleagues are a wonderful thing, but, mentors,
that's where the real work gets done."
— *Junot Diaz*

THE MENTORING RELATIONSHIP

MENTORING IS A RELATIONSHIP, AND LIKE ANY OTHER RELA-tionship, mentoring creates expectations. It is the mentee's responsibility to articulate their expectations. Without that foundational information, the mentoring relationship can lead to miscommunication, confusion, and disappointment, which can ruin the relationship.

Before beginning to examine the mutual expectations, it is imperative to dispel another misconception. Unfortunately, many potential mentees believe being a member of senior leadership is the most significant quality needed to select a mentor. After coming this far in "Mastering Mentoring" you inherently understand that can't be correct ...

The *process* of selecting your Mentor is critically important to your overall success in this journey. Many employees immediately look to the highest members of the organization as their mentor-pool. They see those members and immediately recognize the fruits of a successful career, which is undisputable. What they fail to recognize is a simple "rule of thumb" for selecting a mentor ... select *one two levels higher* than your current position.

This may originally seem counter-intuitive; however, let's pause to think this through. Let's assume you are in the middle of the organization, not a department or division head. You are actively trying to "break the code" to move up in the company. The challenges you have are similar to those of your peers. Further imagine, those in the most senior positions are four to five levels above you, with their challenges immensely different than those of you and your peers. Your first obstacle with selecting a very senior leader is competing for their time. The peers in the top leadership positions expect cancellations and rescheduling. However, this can be very disappointing for the new mentee and often incorrectly believe it was personal. It is also highly probable your issues will be tough for the most senior leaders to relate to. In all likelihood, you will leave your mentoring sessions feeling dissatisfied. Follow the recommended "two levels above" as the starting point for your mentor search.

Most mentees have one common question, "What should I expect from my mentor?" These are several expectations all mentees should expect.

COMMUNICATION AND TIME COMMITMENT

A mentor is expected to initiate conversations, assist in setting goals, and scheduling meetings for the mentoring sessions. The mentee should also expect that the mentor will honesty communicate ideas, thoughts, suggestions, expectations, feedback, and criticism.

The mentor is responsible for creating an environment where the mentee is comfortable and gains confidence and trust when sharing issues and challenges. As a mentor, gaining the trust of the mentee is extremely important, so the mentee freely engages, and authentically shares pertinent information that adds context and clarity to the situation being discussed.

Many people may possess the traits to be good mentors but can't devote the time it demands. A mentor-mentee relationship takes effort from both and without dedication, it won't work. The mentee should expect the mentor to maintain their time commitments. If the mentor cancels the scheduled meetings, or is frequently late, it sends the signal of a lack of interest and investment. The mentee will ultimately lose interest in the relationship. This is why it is the mentor's responsibility to agree to scheduled meetings, ensuring sessions occur without conflict for the mentor.

There is no predetermined amount of time for good mentorship. It depends on the people involved and what it will take to achieve the mentee's goals. The mentor and mentee could meet once a quarter or once a month for lunch. Additionally, the meeting times may change over the duration of the relationship. Ultimately, you and your mentor will jointly decide the schedule that works best.

MENTEES ALSO EXPECT CONNECTIONS AND RESOURCES

A good mentor has spent years developing solid relationships with people and are willing to introduce you to their network. This can expose you to opportunities you may not have had otherwise.

As in all relationships, mentorship isn't one-sided. Mentors also look for mentees with strong networks to expand their professional connections. Therefore, it's important to put time into developing your relationships and growing your network. You never know who may be of interest to a mentor!

Mentors are experienced individuals having established networks within the organization and their given industry. A mentee expects introductions to other senior members who they might not have access to otherwise for their career growth.

If the mentor is an external resource, their network provides access to an entirely different network of professionals. The mentor is expected to connect the mentee with individuals who have the potential to assist in the mentee's development opportunities and career growth. While the mentor is expected to share their network, strong encouragement should be given to the mentee to begin the process of developing their own diverse network. The mentor should provide tips and techniques on thinking about how to grow a network. The mentee probably has one but doesn't realize they have already begun to develop their go-to group of resources.

Mentors are also expected to recommend additional resources to assist in goal achievement. Those resources routinely include books, seminars, additional formal training, etc.

RESPECT FOR THE MENTEE'S CONFIDENTIALITY

Mentees must be able to expect the mentor to maintain their confidentiality and be trustworthy. This is especially critical when both participants are employed within the same organization. The mentor cannot discuss any of the mentee's problems or concerns with anyone else.

Beyond these common mentoring expectations, you and your mentor may develop additional expectations over time that are specific to your relationship.

THE BEST MENTORS SHARE SEVERAL QUALITIES

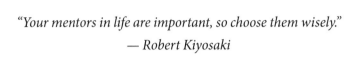

"Your mentors in life are important, so choose them wisely."
— *Robert Kiyosaki*

One of the most common shared qualities of mentors is experience and seniority, but those alone do not provide the qualities a mentee should look for when selecting their mentor. In order to find the best mentor to help you develop professionally, ensure your potential mentor possesses these essential traits.

Enthusiastic

This is one of the most important traits to look for in your mentor. It is important for the mentor to be senior, experienced, wise, etc., but if the mentor is not excited about investing their time in mentorship and its importance to developing the career of an "up and comer", then they are not the best choice. It is also important for the mentor to have a positive impression of the organization or industry where you work. A new mentee does not need a mentor who shares their own complaints and negative insights of the company. The best mentors exude a positive attitude, enthusiasm, and optimism through the good times, as well as the challenging times. These qualities can be inspiring and motivational to the mentee.

Approachable

Similar to enthusiastic, the best mentors share approachability. The best mentors make eye contact, smile, project interest, friendliness, and approach ability. Everyone has observed senior leaders within their organizations that appear brusque, stand-offish, or haughty. They purposefully, or unintentionally, are sending signals that do not welcome you to introduce yourself, much less attempt to get on their schedule. Trust the signals they are sending and look for someone else.

Respects Mentee's Time

The best mentors realize the importance of this effort to the mentee and should invest time determining their availability and then offer that as the basis of the mentoring session schedule. Once that schedule is established, all efforts should be made to honor that time period. Let go of expectations about how often you *should* meet. When meeting with the mentee, avoid distractions such as phones and knocks at the door – keep your focus on the discussion.

Candid and Honest

Mentoring benefits the mentee with the opportunity to receive feedback, and advice, which cannot happen if the mentor lacks candor. Unfortunately, in many organizations, potential mentees find they do not receive career-oriented feedback. Potential reasons include a lack contact with their manager, or their manager lacks skills that enable them to provide honest feedback.

Without feedback, employees have blind spots that can hinder career progression. Finding a good Mentor provides the opportunity to receive feedback from a relatively objective source. Receiving honest feedback, and actionable steps to improve, if necessary, allows the mentee to understand potential developmental areas and increase their self-awareness.

It is also important for the mentor to be transparent and honest about their own experiences. Mentors who are candid about their own shortcomings allow themselves to more relatable to the mentee.

While rare, there are occasions where the mentoring relationship is not working. Be honest when addressing concerns regarding the mentoring relationship. If things are not a good fit, face the facts and follow a no-fault separation policy.

Identifies Weaknesses and Strengths

The best mentors understand everyone has strengths and weaknesses and works to learn what the mentee believes are theirs. Occasionally, they may add to or adjust the mentee's view.

For example, often mentees begin their mentoring relationship believing they are terrible communicators, when in fact, they are not. What they need are proven techniques to improve their communication abilities. A great mentor knows how to help minimize weaknesses and expand strengths to help you fill skill gaps for professional development and growth.

Conversely, often mentees share what they believe to be their strengths. Over time, the mentor may realize what the mentee considers a strength, also needs development.

Just as frequently, a mentee may list communication as a strength, expecting to only address the weaknesses they have shared. However, after several meetings, the mentor notices the mentee frequently interrupts to disagree. That behavior certainly does not represent a strong communication skill. The mentor is expected to identify that as a weakness and work with the mentee to develop a new way of communicating.

Empathetic

It is tough to give honest feedback. It requires incredible communication skills, a thoughtful attitude, and a level of openness that not many people are comfortable sharing. A mentor knows your career progression, your desired path, and your strengths and weaknesses. They can see the gaps that need to be filled to achieve your goals, and they honestly relay them. A mentor is not meant to be a full-time cheerleader, only there to offer encouragement. While a mentor can be a cheerleader at times, their role is to make you better – not just make you *feel* better.

Listens and Reflects

Great mentors understand the importance of active listening and intentional guidance. They ask questions to understand every angle of a situation before offering suggestions. Sometimes, they simply listen.

Mentors who can actively listen and reflect on the information often understand more about you as a person. They know your specific history and situation, so their suggestions are more relevant. Some mentors do not offer any advice and instead continue to ask open-ended questions, which ultimately allows the mentee to arrive at their own conclusions. This method helps the mentee develop problem-solving skills, as well as confidence in decision-making.

Nonjudgmental

Effective mentors have the ability to listen and withhold judgment. In discussing topics, mentors should avoid using loaded words like "should," "must," and "right" or "wrong."

If the mentor is judgmental, it creates distance and the inability for the mentee to honestly share. Conversely, allowing the mentee to be open with their thoughts and feelings is necessary for the mentee's growth.

Constructive Feedback

It is tough to give honest feedback. It requires effective communication skills and a level of openness that not many people are comfortable sharing. Hopefully, at the initial meeting, part of the discussion included how the mentee prefers to receive feedback. Do they want it directly or subtly? Does your mentee want you to provide feedback when you think it is necessary or do they want you to wait until they request it? Realize and respect your mentee might not follow your advice. If your mentee seems skeptical, you may want to suggest a second person's opinion, which also helps your mentee expand his or her network.

Curious

A great mentor has curiosity and a desire to learn and grow. They have the ability to focus on your development as well as their own. They recognize that in order to provide value they must continue to develop their own knowledge, skills, and abilities. The best mentors *want* to know what's going on – in their organization, their field, and with others. These mentors usually have their own mentors and are happy to identify themselves as life-long learners.

If you're looking for a professional mentor, use this list of qualities to help select the right one. For those considering a mentoring role or already in one, it is helpful to reflect on these qualities and find opportunities to improve.

MENTORS ALSO BENEFIT FROM MENTORING

Once a mentor, always a mentor! We see this very often in mentoring; the mentors become so engaged and committed that they keep accepting new mentees. The benefits of mentoring go way beyond the mentee's personal development, often positively affecting the mentors themselves in the process – from supporting inclusion through exposure to new perspectives, to an increased chance of promotion for both parties.

Job Satisfaction

Taking on new or added responsibilities increases job satisfaction. Mentors feel great job satisfaction in helping others grow, in building their network – not only among their colleagues – but also among the younger generations across the organization. This helps mentors also gain a better and different understanding of their organization.

Leadership Skills

Mentoring provides the opportunity for the mentor to "walk the walk" and show their mentees what leadership and executive decision-making looks like in action.

When mentoring others, you gain critical skills to improve as a leader. It reminds the mentor *how* to bring out the best in others, recognize strengths and weaknesses, be diplomatic while getting results, give sound advice and be supportive, and most importantly, how to look within themselves to make changes. As a mentor, you are both a leader and a role model for someone else, and that critical role often pushes you to strive for more; to be more helpful, and simply to be the best version of you.

Mentees frequently ask mentors for advice when tackling new challenges. Effective mentors can share experiences that were successful, as well as ones they wish they had handled differently to help guide mentees. By continuously reflecting on personal experiences to help provide better guidance, mentors can reinforce previously learned leadership skills.

Interpersonal Skills

Interactions with the mentee offer numerous opportunities to practice and refine your interpersonal skills, such as communication, active listening, empathy and patience. Achieving strong interpersonal skills can help develop relationships and collaborate more effectively.

Communication Skills

While mentoring, the mentors need to develop and utilize advanced skill sets in communicating effectively. These include habit management, prioritizing tasks, and an optimal understanding of technology. These skills are integral to effective communication and contribute toward the development and advancement of your hard and soft skills.

Mentoring provides opportunities to leave the comfort zone of your daily communications. It forces the mentor to focus on the *art and skill* of asking questions, delivering feedback, and active listening.

Builds and Reinforces Knowledge

When working with a mentee, you share relevant knowledge gained through your career or experiences and advise them or demonstrate how to perform specific tasks.

For example, you may teach your mentee negotiation methods and practice with them. While the purpose is to help the mentee grow professionally, sharing this knowledge reinforces it within yourself. You may teach them skills you no longer use regularly, so this practice can help you rebuild or strengthen them.

Self-confidence

When your mentee succeeds, you can gain confidence in your skills and abilities. It demonstrates you have qualities that support others' improvement or development.

This confidence boosts your professional and personal self-worth, as well as allows you to feel more assured about your skills and the work you produce. This new or re-gained confidence will display itself in all your endeavors.

Self-reflection

Mentorship provides opportunities to think about and share your experiences. While assessing your positive and negative experiences, you may discover lessons that benefit both you and the mentee. It may also remind you of the positive aspects of your chosen profession.

Exposure to New and Different Perspectives

Mentorship serves as an opportunity to look outside your usual network and potentially connect with someone very different.

For example, your mentee may come from a different background, generation, or part of the organization. When you discuss ideas or situations, there may be different perspectives and approaches. Listening and reflecting upon to your mentee's perspective may help you think differently, discover something, or become aware of new information. These new perspectives can lead to issue resolution, identification for training opportunities, or devising more innovative and creative solutions at work.

Additional Qualifications

Mentors can include mentorship experiences to enhance their resume to differentiate from other candidates. This experience demonstrates you have valuable knowledge to share, communication skills, and investment in the company. Participating in mentorship opportunities also shows you the value of building relationships and helping others develop professionally.

Professional Network

Everyone knows the old saying, "It is who you know, not what you know." While building a network of trusted peers is advice typically given to mentees, mentors benefit from the same.

One of the benefits of mentoring is the opportunity to rekindle old relationships and develop new ones that could lead to unique opportunities and insights. For example, if a mentee asks a question about an area in which you are less familiar, or they want to build a skill you do not possess, reaching out to a colleague to help your mentee affords the opportunity to learn from a peer and strengthen your own professional network.

PERSONAL REFLECTION:

Circle areas of expertise where you believe you could mentor someone else

Communication	Goal Development	Technology
Financial Management	Financial Management	Contracts
Labor Relations	Project Management	Problem Solving
Strategic Planning	Time Management	Logistics
Conflict Resolution	Resume Review	Public Speaking

Let's further capture your thoughts by responding to the below questions.

Why do you feel you have expertise? Do you have a note-worthy experience that adds credence to your competency in that area?

_____

_____

_____

_____

_____

_____

_____

What are your concerns regarding mentoring in that area?

_____

_____

_____

_____

_____

_____

_____

Additional thoughts:

_____

_____

_____

_____

_____

_____

_____

EXPECTATIONS FOR MENTEES

"Believe in yourself and all that you are. Know that there is something inside of you that is greater than any obstacle."
— *Christian Larson*

In many ways, a successful mentoring relationship is based on expectation fulfillment. The mentee enters into the relationship with numerous expectations of their mentor. For the relationship to succeed, the mentee must realize the mentor is agreeing to participate with their own expectations of the mentee. The relationship works best when both participants are aware of the expectations prior to agreeing to the mentoring relationship. Prior to entering a mentoring relationship, the mentee needs to consider their ability to:

- Take the initiative in the relationship. Be prepared with topics to discuss, ask for what you need. Use email, phone, and time in person.
- Drive the mentoring relationship. Assume you mentor is very busy and be the person to first initiate and continuously contact your mentor, as well as respond to all communications in a timely manner. One tip is to always end each meeting with the question, "when should we meet next?" in order to get a date on the calendar after comparing both of your schedules.
- Approach your mentoring partnership with respect, professionalism and an open mind.
- Be honest about your expectations of the mentoring relationship.
- Commit to the goals you want to achieve with the assistance of your mentor.

- Bring questions, confusions, concerns, and problems. But also bring successes, alternatives, and ideas.
- Meet as often as is appropriate. Scheduling in advance, spontaneously, or a combination of the two are all fine – as long as they work with both parties.
- Be clear about what you need, and if an activity or suggestion just isn't of interest, simply state you are not interested.
- Do not expect your mentor to know everything or be able to help in every situation but do seek your mentor's advice early if an issue arises.
- Ask for information and, if appropriate, advice. Understand that any *advice* is not *direction* and may not be right for you. The more important a concern, the more important to weigh advice carefully and get second and third opinions.
- Be open to discussions and constructive alternative ways to handle issues and responsibilities.
- Be receptive to suggestions and feedback from your mentor. During your initial meeting, honestly communicate how you prefer to receive feedback.
- Recognize, with the right Mentor, criticisms will only be offered in an effort to help you grow professionally.
- Elicit a mentor's help in developing other informal supportive relationships.
- Be honest about any minor concerns regarding the mentoring relationship too. If things are just not working, face facts and follow a "no fault" separation policy; you can get a new mentor or just use informal support.
- Focus on achieving goals. Keep your goals and those of your mentor in mind during every interaction. Remind yourself of the goals you set out to accomplish; this will help you keep track of your progress.

- Engage in a growth mindset.
- Create SMART goals that will contribute to your development. Although further defined later in this book, SMART is the abbreviation for Specific goals; Measurable goals; Achievable goals; Realistic goals and Timely goals.
- Be authentic, open, and honest.
- Prepare for all mentoring meetings.
- Be willing to stretch and step out of your comfort zone.
- Ask for (and give!) specific feedback.
- Focus on the future.
- Be mindful of when your mentoring partnership has reached its natural end. If all the goals have been achieved, then it may be time to find another mentor to address the next set of goals. You also have the option to continue to meet with your current mentor and develop the next set of goals together. Additionally, you can simply thank your mentor and move on to start another mentoring partnership. It is strongly encouraged to stay in touch with your mentor and keep them updated on your progress as you move through your career. Please note, some amazing mentor matches may last a lifetime!

Clker.com

MUTUAL MENTORING EXPECTATIONS: SUMMARY

Use this summary to ensure your expectations are realistic, and the mentoring relationship has a solid foundation for the mentee to achieve their goals.

Keep Communications Open

MENTOR: Help your mentee set realistic expectations.

MENTEE: Be honest and candid. Let your mentor know the goals you want to achieve.

Offer Support

MENTOR: Encourage communication and participation. Help create a solid plan of action.

MENTEE: Remember your mentor is there for you, but only as a guide.

Define Expectations

MENTOR: Help set up a system to measure achievement.

MENTEE: Review your goals. Make sure your mentor knows what to expect from you

Maintain Contact

MENTOR: Respond to your e-mails in a timely fashion. Answer questions and provide advice, resources, and guidance when appropriate.

MENTEE: Be polite and courteous. Keep up with your e-mails and ask questions.

Be Honest

MENTOR: Be truthful in your evaluations, but also tactful.

MENTEE: Let your mentor know if you do not understand something or have a differing opinion.

Actively Participate

MENTOR: Engage in your own learning while you are mentoring, collaborate on projects, and ask questions and experiment.

MENTEE: Listen and learn. Ask if you can observe your mentor's work if they are local.

Be Innovative and Creative

MENTOR: Share your ideas, give advice and be a resource for new concepts.

MENTEE: Offer ideas on what activities and exercises you can do together.

Get to Know Each Other

MENTOR and **Mentee:** Remember that people come from diverse backgrounds and experiences. Get to know each other on an individual basis.

Be Reliable and Consistent

MENTOR and **Mentee:** The more consistent you are, the more you will be trusted.

Stay Positive

MENTOR: Recognize the work the protégé has done and the progress made.

MENTEE: Remember that your mentor is offering feedback to be helpful and not criticizing.

SELECTING A MENTOR

"When selecting a mentor, we must be aware
of what we want from them."
– Russell Brand

It is time. You've recognized the benefits of entering into a mentoring rela-tionship and are ready to receive assistance is attaining your professional goals or overcoming a skill gap or challenge. Congratulations!

Assess Timing

Think about where you are in your career and identify the reasons why you want a mentor. Reflect on your personal attributes, what you think you may be like as a mentee and how you prefer to accept feedback.

Identify Mentorship Goals

Determine what you hope to learn from your mentor. Consider outlining the goals you have set for your professional growth. Being able to artic-ulate your objectives provides a starting point for who to consider as a mentor and topics to consider for your initial conversations.

Why is goal setting critical to the mentoring process? Goal setting is a powerful driver of motivation and learning. Goals provide clear direction, allowing the mentee to take small actions to ultimately achieve their main objective.

Measurable goals are tremendously motivating, Mentees can visibly see progress toward the objective as they hit each milestone and short-term goal. This helps mentees remain engaged, as they close in on their final objective.

Goals improve accountability. The mentee is responsible for completing the actions for each milestone. While the mentor is there to assist, the responsibility and accountability is that of the mentee.

Goals help reveal obstacles. Mentees can compare their performance with the desired outcome. This approach helps mentees discover where they are falling short and where they are thriving; revealing what needs to be improved or adjusted.

Awareness

When reviewing the qualities and expectations of mentors, let us think of senior leaders within your organization who you already know. Think about people you respect in your career field who you have worked with or met by attending meetings. A good guide to selecting a mentor at the right level of leadership is to identify people *two levels* above your current position.

New mentees often make the common mistake of wanting to engage with the highest leaders of the organization. While they certainly possess organizational expertise, they are too far removed from the issues impacting junior employees and will be unable to provide the on-going time and attention you should reasonably expect.

Additional Options

If no one from the senior leaders you already know excite you, start asking peers what senior leaders they know and admire. Continue the conversation by asking for a description of the qualities that make them admirable. Ask others if they are familiar with that same individual. Once you have received several informal endorsements, add the senior leaders them to your list.

Another method for finding potential mentors includes professional organizations or networking events. These options introduce you to potential candidates, but they do not provide important information related to reputation and credibility.

Prepare

When reviewing the list of potential mentors, think about your personality and communication style. What kind of mentor would best complement you? Purposefully decide if you want to choose someone who's your opposite (an extrovert to your introvert, for example), or someone who's personality is similar to yours.

When you have a consolidated list of several potential mentors, develop a short professional biography; include education and positions you have held throughout the organization. Incorporate awards or letters of appreciation. Succinctly state the goals you want to achieve or the issue you want to overcome. Be prepared to leave this information with the potential mentor.

PERSONAL REFLECTION:

What expectations do you have for your mentor or mentee?

_____

_____

_____

_____

_____

_____

_____

What qualities are you looking for in a mentor?

_____

_____

_____

_____

_____

_____

_____

Potential mentors that immediately come to mind:

_____

_____

_____

_____

_____

_____

What are some of your career goals or current professional challenges you are experiencing?

_____

_____

_____

_____

_____

_____

CHAPTER 6:

THE INITIAL MEETING... AND THOSE THAT FOLLOW

"A good mentor hopes you move on. A great mentor knows you will."
— Leslie Higgins (a main character featured on the TV show Ted Lasso)

INITIAL MEETING

FOLLOW THE NORMAL PROCEDURES FOR GETTING ON THEIR calendar. Do not be disappointed if the meeting is scheduled a couple weeks away. For the day of the initial meeting, dress professionally – similarly to how you would dress for an interview. In many ways you *are* interviewing.

Be conscious of the time allotted for your meeting, usually this initial meeting is scheduled for 30 minutes. It is recommended to develop and bring bulleted talking points for the information you want to cover, to help ensure you stay on track.

Start by explaining why you believe a mentoring relationship is needed at this time and what you expect of the relationship. Name the reasons you are interested in them as your mentor. Do not be afraid to let the mentor know you asked throughout the organization, and they came highly recommended.

Referring to your notes, share your goal(s) or objectives. Be specific.

The potential mentor may ask several questions as you share your information. They are assessing if you are a good "fit" for them, as you are deciding if they are a good "fit" for you. The mentor may be trying to learn more about a mentee's current expertise and skills to determine if their expertise aligns in the areas of the mentee's objectives.

The potential mentor may also ask questions about your career goals and past to identify the mentee's long-term desires. Questions mentors commonly ask are as follows:

What does success look like to you?

This question helps learn about the mentee's values and priorities. Success can be defined numerous ways, so the mentee's responses highlight what they consider valuable.

Where do you see yourself in five years?

This question is very popular, this informs the potential mentor about the mentee's goals. The response helps the potential mentor design their support to image a path forward to help the mentee reach that destination.

What do you hope to gain from the mentoring sessions?

The mentee's response helps clarify a specific goal, a career path, a skill, or an issue. Some mentees may not be completely sure, which also helps the mentor understand efforts are needed to help the mentee articulate objectives. Avoid not having an objective, if you can.

What is an obstacle you're currently facing?

The response identifies what the mentee considers challenging. This helps the mentor know if efforts would be required to assist in overcoming specific challenges or the mentee's areas of sensitivity.

If you could learn a new professional skill, what would it be?

This provides the opportunity for the mentee to be creative, inform their mentor about their interests, or identify a professional weakness. This can help a mentor determine types of advice, and recommendations for job opportunities.

Have you ever quit a job? If so, why?

When a mentee identifies a specific challenge at one of their previous jobs that caused them to leave, it helps the mentor assess aspects of the mentee's personality or workplace values.

Who do you talk to about workplace challenges and successes?

This reveals the mentee's support system. It helps the mentor identify potential discussion areas that may include turning to their peers or coworkers for support.

Many mentors ask additional questions that fit in the following categories:

Career journey: These specific questions replace the general, "Tell me about your career."

- What was your educational experience?
- What was your first job?
- What led you to your current career path?
- Did you plan to have this career path, or did it just happen?

Mentee, as a person: Not too personal, but to learn more about them and what is important.

- Where did you learn your current values?
- Do you have any role models you look up to or people you admire?
- What do you love to do outside of work?
- What inspires you?

Understanding their goals: Provides clarity to their career aspirations.

- What are your short-term goals?
- What are your long-term goals?
- What interested you about having a mentor?
- What areas of your life do you want to grow?
- What skills do you want to develop?
- If you could go back in time, would you choose a different career?

Strengths and weaknesses: These questions help identify the Mentee's self-awareness and level of candor.

- What do you consider to be your strengths?
- In what areas do you think you need to improve?
- Does your current role help you leverage your strengths?
- What parts of your job do your weaknesses hinder you?
- How do you mitigate your weaknesses?

Challenge addresses: Not every mentee is looking for goal achievement. Sometimes a mentee is trying to overcome a challenge or professional issue. Similar to the ones specifically aimed at goal clarification, these are used to help the mentee explain the situation.

- What's a challenge you're currently facing in your career?
- What ideas have you developed to help you overcome challenges and meet your goals?

- What obstacles do you see that might prevent you from achieving your goals?
- What will you do differently tomorrow to meet those challenges?
- How could a mentor support you in overcoming your challenges?

Reflect and express gratitude: Thankfulness is a vital life skill. It helps focus on the good things, rather than on the things we feel we are lacking. These help the mentee to pause and identify positives in their career or life.

- What makes you feel really grateful?
- Who is someone you are grateful for in your life? What have they given you?
- What was a period in your life or career where you felt like you had the most growth?

Throughout this discussion and the sessions that follow, it is important the mentor allows the mentee time to think without speaking to fill the silence. Many mentors are not comfortable with "lags of silence" and rush into the conversation to avoid it.

To help avoid rushing in to filling the void, mentors need to practice the following:

- Pay attention to the thinker. Listen with respect, interest, and curiosity.
- Keep your eyes on their face; do not look away.
- Look interested and be interested.
- Occasionally make sounds to indicate understanding or encouragement.
- Be at ease.
- Smile occasionally, when it won't be interpreted as derision.
- Do not allow yourself to interrupt.

- Do not ask picky, clarifying or confirming questions.
- When your mentee has nothing more to say, ask, "Is there anything else you think or feel or want to say about this?"
- Watch their body language. If the mentee becomes quiet, but their eyes are alive, relax and stay silent – they're thinking.

After some amount of questioning, toward the end of the session, the mentor may decide to accept your mentoring request. Some mentors tell the mentee they will provide a response within a certain amount of time. In either instance, the next consideration is developing a meeting schedule. The standard is either 30 or 60 minutes each quarter. If the mentee is experiencing a professional conflict or issue, the schedule may be more frequent.

Do not forget to leave your bio, the mentor will want to refer to it when planning the agenda for the next meeting.

Finally, if you ask someone to be your mentor and that person refuses, do not be hurt or offended. This is not personal! Senior leaders are typically extremely busy and the ones who have previously mentored understand the time commitment.

If the potential mentor declines, simply thank them for their time and ask for a referral. They have heard your mentoring objectives and should be able to recommend someone with the professional qualities to achieve your goals.

There is no singular method for selecting a mentor. Not everyone wants to be a mentor, nor does seniority and responsibilities automatically qualify a person to be a mentor. Even in companies where there is an established mentor program, you invest the time to research, compose of list of potentials, identify your objectives, and create your biography. Meet with several, and then select a mentor who you like, is easy to talk to, will give you honest advice, and help you achieve your goals.

THE SECOND MEETING: DEVELOPING THE PARTNERSHIP PLAN

The second meeting sets the tone for future meetings. In this meeting, the recommendation is to discuss a structured accountability process. The mentor and mentee discuss each other's expectations. Usually, the mentee is expected to develop the agenda, send a copy in advance and come prepared with the outline of what to discuss. This provides the mentee responsibility for guiding the mentoring meeting. It usually also increases the mentee's engagement in the outcome of each session.

The mentor uses this time to explain to the mentee they are going to have to work if they want results and see progress and let them know you expect them to come prepared for every meeting and share the schedule in advance.

The meeting schedule frequency is confirmed, and the goals may be reiterated. The important topics of the second meeting may include: Mentee's preferred learning style, establishing ground rules for future sessions, and creating a "Partnership Plan" to keep the relationship focused.

Some mentors want to keep the sessions more formal, scheduling them in their office or a conference room. Other mentors may set a more informal tone and schedule meetings at lunch, in a convenient restaurant or café.

Growing the Relationship

In the beginning of the meeting, most mentors may invest a few minutes in casual conversation in an effort to relax and get to know you.

Determining Desired Outcomes

Next, the conversation turns to establishing the basic goals, which can be initially broad, but will be narrowed down in subsequent meetings to reflect the mentee's specific professional objectives.

Clearly Identify Responsibilities

After identifying the goals, address the specifics of what aspects of goal achievement the mentor and the mentee are responsible for doing. Responsibilities state which areas each participant takes accountability. State these responsibilities clearly so there is no mistaking each person's role.

- For example, the mentee may write something like, "As mentee, I am responsible for seeking opportunities and experiences to enhance my learning, communicating and reviewing my progress regularly with my mentor."
- The mentor might write, "As mentor, I agree to provide support and encouragement, provide feedback on progress, and meet regularly."

Create Ground Rules

These are established to ensure maximum success of each session and for the relationship as a whole. Often those include:

- Establish and maintain a meeting schedule.
- Reschedule any missed meetings.
- Respect each other's opinions.
- Maintain confidentiality.
- Provide honest feedback.
- Provide criticism constructively.
- Work diligently toward goal achievement.
- No-fault termination of mentoring relationship.

Identify Outside Activities that Assist in Goal Attainment

This may include books, videos, training, or workshops. Often the mentor will include invites to the mentee for meetings the mentor is attending as learning opportunities and exposure.

Progress Evaluation

Regular progress reviews help to ensure progress is occurring. If you are the mentor, evaluate your mentee once every six months. If you are the mentee, suggest an evaluation every six months and include it in your plan. During the sixth month review, the mentor and mentee should revisit the mentorship plan, goals, and objectives to review what has been accomplished or develop new goals and objectives.

Make Adjustments as Needed

After reviewing the mentorship plan together, make adjustments to the plan as needed, such as changing goal completion dates, modifying goals, or adding new goals. Use the notes that the mentor made during review and any concerns the mentee stated to adjust the plan.

For example, if the mentee set a goal to attend three professional development workshops within the next year, but have only found two suitable ones, simply adjust the goal or consider it met. Or, if the mentee has already accomplished their two-year goals at the one-year evaluation, set a new goal to work toward.

No-fault Termination

This is used if either party determines the relationship is not achieving its intended results, the mentoring relationship can be dissolved. Either participant should first identify the issues and try to resolve them. If no resolution is possible, request a no-fault termination. Sign, date and provide each participant a copy.

SAMPLE MENTORING PARTNERSHIP AGREEMENT #1

We have agreed on the following goals and objectives as the focus of this mentoring relationship:

- To develop a dynamic reciprocal relationship fostering professional growth.
- To work toward the development of a career development plan.
- To introduce the mentee/protégé to best practices.

We have discussed the process by which we will work together, develop, and, in that same spirit of partnership, collaborate on the development of a work plan. In order to ensure that our relationship is a mutually rewarding and satisfying experience for both of us, we agree to:

1. MEET REGULARLY. OUR SPECIFIC SCHEDULE OF CONTACT AND MEETINGS, INCLUDING ADDITIONAL MEETINGS, IS AS FOLLOWS:

We will meet once a month and be in contact by telephone or e-mail at least every two weeks.

2. LOOK FOR MULTIPLE OPPORTUNITIES AND EXPERIENCES TO ENHANCE THE PROTÉGÉ'S LEARNING.

We have identified, and will commit to, the following specific opportunities and venues for learning:

- Protégé will attend faculty meetings. We will meet prior to each meeting and debrief following each meeting.
- Protégé will attend a
  _____ with mentor.
- Protégé and mentor will attend faculty forum meetings.

3. MAINTAIN CONFIDENTIALITY OF OUR RELATIONSHIP.

Confidentiality for us means that what we discuss remains between us. Mentor and protégé will agree ahead of time if specific information is to be shared with anyone else.

4. HONOR THE GROUND RULES WE HAVE DEVELOPED FOR THE RELATIONSHIP.

Our ground rules include:

- We will meet after work hours.
- Protégé will assume responsibility for confirming meetings.
- Protégé will pay for own expenses.
- At the conclusion of each meeting, we will target topics for discussion at the next session.

5. PROVIDE REGULAR FEEDBACK TO EACH OTHER AND EVALUATE PROGRESS. WE WILL ACCOMPLISH THIS BY:

Reviewing career goals once a month, discussing progress, and checking in with each other regularly for the first month to make sure our individual needs are being met in the relationship, and periodically thereafter.

We agree to meet regularly until we have accomplished our predefined goals or for a maximum of 12 months. At the end of this period of time, we will review this agreement, evaluate our progress, and reach a conclusion. The relationship then will be considered complete. If we choose to continue our mentoring partnership, we may negotiate a basis for continuation, so long as we have stipulated the mutually agreed-on goals.

In the event one of us believes it is no longer productive for us to continue or the situation is compromised, we may decide to seek outside intervention or conclude the relationship. In this event, we agree to use closure as a learning opportunity.

_____   _____
Mentor's Signature and Date   Mentee's Signature and Date

MENTORING PARTNERSHIP PLAN

Mentee Name: _____

Office Phone: _____

Email: _____

Mentor: _____

Office Phone: _____

Email: _____

We have agreed on the following goals and objectives as the focus of this mentoring relationship:

    1.

    2.

    3.

We have discussed the process by which we will work together, develop, and, in that same spirit of partnership, collaborate on the development of a work plan. In order to ensure our relationship is a mutually rewarding and satisfying experience for both of us, we agree to:

Meeting frequency: _____

Responsibilities:

As Mentor, I am responsible to:

As Mentee, I am responsible to:

Ground Rules:

_____

_____

_____

_____

_____

_____

_____

Long term goals:

_____

_____

_____

_____

_____

_____

_____

Short term goals:

_____

_____

_____

_____

_____

_____

_____

Skills to develop:

_____

_____

_____

_____

_____

_____

_____

EVALUATION OF MENTEE PROGRESS:

The following has been accomplished in the last six months:

_____

_____

_____

_____

_____

_____

_____

No-fault Termination

This is used if either party determines the relationship is not achieving its intended results, the mentoring relationship can be dissolved. Either participant should first identify the issues and try to resolve them. If no resolution is possible, request a no-fault termination.

_____

Mentor's Signature and Date

_____

Mentee's Signature and Date

As you can see, the second meeting is critical, in addition to discussion and working together to create the mentoring partnership plan (or mentoring agreement), this is the first opportunity for the mentor and mentee to work closely together. Participants usually leave this meeting tired, but with a sense of accomplishment and excitement.

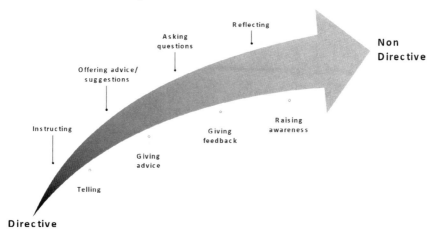

realbalancewellness.wordpress.com/2016/09/13/
client-centered-directiveness-an-oxymoron-that-works-part-one

MENTORING MEETINGS

Every mentoring meeting requires essential topics of discussion along with challenges and solutions that contribute to the overall goals of the mentee to make sure that progress is being made. Thoroughly articulating the goals is critical for the mentor's understanding and the mentee's success.

It is usually during the third or fourth meeting where the mentor introduces the mentee to the SMART technique of goal setting. The SMART Technique is one of many methods as well as one of the most common.

SMART GOALS

Each element of the SMART framework creates a carefully planned, clear and trackable goals. The SMART process defines goals using five principles:

1. SPECIFIC: goals clearly highlight what you want to achieve
2. MEASURABLE: goals have metrics attached to them
3. ACHIEVABLE: goals are ambitious but not unachievable
4. REALISTIC: goals are attainable with the available resources
5. TIMELY: goals have a reasonable deadline

Attempting to create goals previously may not have aided your success because they were too general or difficult to achieve. It is nearly impossible to work toward or track a poorly written goal.

Your original goal may have been written as, "I want to be in leadership." While this may be a true statement, it is incredibly broad. Utilizing the SMART technique helps evolve this statement into something actionable and achievable.

S – SPECIFIC

Being clear, detailed, and narrow in scope helps you visualize the steps required to achieve your goal.

Example: "I want to earn a position managing a development team for a startup tech company."

M – MEASURABLE

In our example, the goal is to earn a position managing a development team for a startup tech company. You must be able to assess your progress. One way would be to track the number of management positions you have applied for or interviews you have completed. Creating measurable milestones provide the opportunity to evaluate and course-correct if needed. It is important to reward yourself as you accomplish milestones.

Example: "I will apply to three open manager of a development team positions at tech startups."

A – ACHIEVABLE

Using our example, before you create your goal, honestly assess if you have the knowledge, skills, abilities, and credentials to compete for the management position. Before you begin working toward a goal, decide whether it is something you can achieve now or whether there are additional preliminary steps that need to be accomplished.

Example: "I will update my resume with my latest certification, so I can apply to three open manager of a development team positions at tech startups."

R – RELEVANT

Review your goal to ensure it works toward your broader objectives. Validate the reason the goal is important and how achieving it will help you achieve your long-term goals.

Example: "To achieve my goal of being in leadership, I will update my resume with my latest certification, so I may apply to three open manager of a development team positions at tech startups."

T – TIME-BASED

You will want to give your goal a time period for achievement. For example, if your goal is to earn a promotion to a senior position, you might give yourself six months. If you have not achieved your goal by then, take time to consider why. Your timeframe might have been unrealistic, you might have run into obstacles, or your goal might have been unachievable.

Example: "To achieve my goal of being in leadership, I will update my resume with my latest certification so I can apply to three open manager of a development team positions at tech startups this week."

SMART goal techniques create boundaries, define the required steps, identify resources necessary, and develop milestones that indicate progress. Using SMART goals helps ensure you reach your goal efficiently and effectively.

SMART GOALS

S
SPECIFIC

What do you want to accomplish?

M
MEASURABLE

How do you plan to track your progress?

A
ACHIEVABLE

Is this goal realistic and achievable? How do you plan to achieve it?

R
RELEVANT

How relevant is this goal to you?

T
TIMEBOUND

How long will it take to achieve this goal?>

For the success of the mentorship, it is critical for the mentees to be prepared and following an agenda makes it is easier to initiate the conversation and ensure the session remains on track.

To prepare the agenda, the mentee may reflect on the professional goals previously shared and how they can be incorporated as the topics of discussion. In preparing the agenda, remember to ask your mentor if they have anything they want included.

As the mentor, upon receipt of the agenda, it is best to note any related experiences that may give valuable perspective to the mentee. Try to always include any tips or techniques you have previously successfully used.

MENTOR MEETING AGENDA

Although it is recommended the mentee take responsibility for preparing the meeting plan, it is not mandatory. Occasionally, the mentor will have specific discussion topics or activities. Regardless of who prepares the agenda, it should follow a similar pattern.

Build Rapport

Mentor-mentee relationships work best when there is honesty and openness. However, it is often difficult to be open before you have built trust. Every mentoring session should dedicate time at the beginning to getting to know each other. This is important, especially in the beginning of the relationship.

One of the easiest ways to build rapport for the mentor and mentee is to share professional stories. These exchanges allow the mentee to gain valuable insights from a different and more experienced perspective. This also provides an opportunity for the mentors to learn about their mentees, their responsibilities, insights, and opinions.

Skill-Related Topics

Discussing skill-related topics is a great way to spend time with your mentor. Consider talking about areas the mentor already possesses that you want to develop and improve. For example:

- How do I improve my public speaking skills?
- What do you think are my three best skills?
- What skill area do you think I should improve?
- What skills do you think are the most beneficial for me to attain for my current position?

Career story topics

Talk to your mentor about their personal career journey. Get their insights on what the organization was like when they first started or what lessons they learned at the beginning of their career.

- What was your first industry job?
- How did you reach your current position?
- Do you have any regrets about your career choices?
- Did you ever make a mistake in a job, and how did you demonstrate resiliency?

Feedback Topics

Feedback is a gift! Feedback is a constructive method for improvement. To help you grow professionally, you want your mentor's insights on your current performance, a project you manage, a written report or presentation you gave. Ask for your mentor's feedback and take notes on what was said.

- How would you rate my presentation?
- Do you think I am ready to apply for a promotion?
- How do you think others perceive me in my new role?

Situational Advice Topics

Open discussions to include receiving your mentor's perspective on an issue you are facing. It helps you get immediate responses to questions you have about your job or responsibilities.

- How should I handle downsizing in my department?
- I am having trouble getting a team member to submit assignments on time. How do I proactively address this?
- How do I ask my boss for a raise?

Discuss Mentoring Topics

The choice of agenda topics for mentees should flow directly from their goals. It often helps to prepare specific questions to ask your mentor beforehand.

With respect to goal achievement, what is working for you and what is not working for you? Consider personal and external factors. Be honest and do not make excuses. This is a great opportunity to receive valuable advice from an experienced and successful leader. You should feel comfortable and safe sharing your challenges.

Also consider discussing what skills, behaviors and beliefs you want to improve to be able effectively execute current responsibilities and achieve your goals. As the mentoring relationship progresses, another recommendation for the start of the meeting is to review progress or share new challenges. A quick way to begin to review for the discussion includes:

- What have I accomplished toward goal achievement since last session?
- What did I plan to do, but not yet accomplish?
- Are there new challenges or opportunities I have identified since last session?
- How do I feel I am progressing? Is there anything we need to do differently?

While most mentoring sessions focus on discussion, the mentor can expose their mentee through numerous activities. Activities can be categorized as basic, intermediate or advanced, and can be shared progressively as your mentee grows professionally. Mentors can use the list below to discuss with their mentees or assign actions for between sessions.

MENTORING ACTIVITIES

Basic Activities:

- **Mini workshop.** Select one of the skills your mentee would like to develop and lead a mini workshop focused on improving that skill in particular. Common areas include public speaking or time management. Draw upon your own personal experiences or invite a colleague to expose your mentee to your professional network.
- **Career mapping:** Does your mentee have a planned path for career advancement? If not, help them create one. Map out the knowledge, skills, and abilities they will have to achieve to progress in their career field.
- **Observe others in meetings**. Ask them to identify any differences they note between senior leaders and their peers.
- **Gather information.** Attend lectures, watch videos, and read articles on subjects related to their goals.

Intermediate Activities:

- **Job shadow.** Recommend a senior leader in the organization for the mentee to follow throughout the business day.
- **Resume review.** Use your expertise to review their resume and make needed changes.

- **Practice presentations.** Have your mentee bring a presentation they are tasked with giving, listen to them and provide feedback.
- **Training.** Recommend training or workshops for your mentee to attend.

Advanced Activities:

- **Prepare for a promotion interview.** Perform a "mock interview" with your mentee, which includes interview questions from their next level. Provide feedback.
- **Mentor others.** It may be time for your mentee to put into action what they have learned throughout their mentoring relationship; time to pay-it-forward by mentoring someone else.
- **Make a professional recommendation.** Is your mentee aware of a process that is ineffective or inefficient? Work with your mentee to prepare the process change discussion with their manager.

Close the mentoring session by summarizing what was discussed. It is often helpful to share what you considered the most important information you learned, or advice you received.

At the end of every meeting, create an action list for the mentee, with both of you agreeing on the tasks that need to be completed for the next mentoring session. This action allows the mentee to have a clear understanding and focus on the tasks they need to complete, simultaneously holding the mentee accountable for achieving their goals.

Finally, establish the habit that the mentee shares the most meaningful topic, advice or activity from the current session. This provides immediate feedback to both of you by identifying what was the most valuable.

Featuring Mr. Mark Mhley, Navy Veteran, Founder and CEO of Re4ormed, and Ms. Adrienne Somerville, CEO of Technical Solutions Corporation and Somerville Consulting Group, LLC, April 29, 2021, Washington, DC

SAMPLE MEETING AGENDA

It is also efficient to have a consistent format for the mentoring sessions. Below is a sample agenda to guide your time together.

1. **Warm-up and check-in**: Initially, this is the part of the session devoted to getting to know each other. As the relationship progresses, this may evolve to a personal check-in or update on how everything is going.

2. **Check on action progress since the last session**: What were the results of taking a particular action? What has the mentee learned or accomplished? What went well? What could have been done differently?

3. **Review the topics for the current session**: The mentee should have included one to three items they want to discuss in the session. Ideally, the mentee should have sent identified challenges and priorities to you before the session. They may choose something from their original goals or identify a new goal they want to achieve.

4. **Identify solutions for addressing those challenges**: Discuss potential ways of resolving challenges and determining actions to take immediate steps.

5. **Prioritize the actions to take between now and the next session**: Narrow actions to no more than three and make them specific and realistic.

IMGBIN.COM

INVEST IN YOUR MENTORING CONNECTION

There are proactive steps Mentees can take to ensure the connection to their mentor begins in a positive manner and remains positive throughout the relationship. The following actions cannot be overly stressed:

- **Prepare:** Respect your mentor's time by coming prepared to all sessions. Have an outline of the questions or statements related to the meeting's agenda you want to cover.
- **Be interested:** Show interest in your mentor as a person. Ask questions about their life, career and interests. You may want to ask about their education, training, and current

responsibilities. Do not hesitate to ask your mentor about their opinion on professional topics or efforts occurring across the organization.

- **Take notes:** Note the advice, information, or actions your Mentor has given you. This allows you to summarize key points from the session and confirm upcoming actions.

- **Ask about their goals:** Mentees are often surprised to learn why their mentor agreed to participate in a mentoring relationship. Ask if they have any goals they are hoping to achieve as well.

- **Share:** Build a stronger bond with your mentor by sharing what you learned from the outside activities related to your goals. Provide honest feedback regarding their value. Include points or topics you found interesting, and why.

- **Follow through:** When your mentor makes suggestions, implement them. If it requires additional knowledge, look for ways to learn outside of the session. This demonstrates you listen to their advice and respect their opinion enough to take action.

- **Respect their time:** Remember your mentor has responsibilities outside of mentoring. Respect inherent boundaries by trying to hold discussions until the scheduled meeting time. Try to resolve issues on you own, and then report the effectiveness of your actions during the next meeting. If your mentor has shared their cell phone number, think very carefully about the purpose and urgency before making a call.

- **Give credit:** As your skills increase, a manager or colleague may notice and compliment you. Let them know you are in a mentoring relationship, tell them your mentor's name, and mention they helped you learn those skills.

- **Say thank you:** Let your mentor know you appreciate their time and advice by saying thank you frequently. Occasionally, you may want to write a "thank you" note. Mentors like to hear their efforts are noticed and appreciated!

PERSONAL REFLECTION:

Mentee, begin drafting the information for your first meeting. Reflect and write your thoughts on:

- Why mentoring now?
- Why are you asking this potential mentor?
- Professional journey
- Long-term goals
- Your strengths and weaknesses
- Current challenges
- Beyond great expectations

Goals For A Mentor-Mentee Relationship

Mentor

- Validate the mentor's leadership skills.
- Become recognized as an advisor throughout the company.
- Learn to clearly communicate.
- Expand their understanding of new perspectives.
- Find hidden talent for potential promotions or leadership roles.

Mentee

- Learn the workplace culture.
- Excellerate skills development.
- Networking opportunities.
- Career advise or professional development.

https://www.togetherplatform.com/blog/
objectives-and-goals-for-your-workplace-mentoring-program

_____

_____

_____

_____

_____

_____

Initiation	Negotiations	Development & Action	Closure
Mentor and mentee matching and induction, scoping parameters of the relationship, clarifying roles, stating commitment, agreeing on mentorship logistics, establishing ground rules	Negotiated and detailed planning which results in defined learning goals, objectives, success measures (deliverables), action plans, activities, learning strategies and reflective processes, responsibilities, accountability	Ongoing and completed actions and achievement, iterative review and development of new objectives and actions, ongoing evaluation of outcomes of relationship	Relationship concludes, celebration, summative evaluation

Researchgate.net

CHAPTER 7:

TRANSITIONING THE MENTOR-MENTEE RELATIONSHIP

"A truly great mentor is hard to find, difficult to part with, and impossible to forget."
— Lucia Ballas Traynor

EVERY MENTORING LIFE CYCLE CONSISTS OF FOUR PHASES:

Phase 1: Purpose

THE PURPOSE OR PREPARATION PHASE BEGINS WHEN A PERSON realizes they want to find a mentor. This phase is characterized by an interest to learn and a desire to succeed. The mentee begins a process to search for an individual who can fulfill this professional goal.

Focus areas of this phase include:

- Recognizing a mentoring relationship would positively impact your career

- Being highly motivated and proactive
- Wanting to learn as much as possible in a short period of time
- Having conversations to learn about potential mentors

This phase completes when the mentor agrees to enter a mentoring relationship with the mentee.

Phase 2: Engagement and Agreement Definition

Once a mentee has found a mentor, the engagement phase begins. In this phase, the relationship is built and trust is established. The focus during this time is on creating a positive connection between mentor and mentee.

This phase includes:

- Building rapport and trust
- Discussing goals, progress, and challenges
- Focusing on the relationship, not just the task or project at hand
- Spending time getting to know each other as people, not just professionals
- Setting boundaries around expectations and communication

The mentor is responsible for setting boundaries and parameters, to avoid any confusion or resentment later in the relationship.

During this phase, important questions for the participants to discuss include duration of relationship, frequency of meetings, and expectations.

Phase 3: Growth

Most of the mentoring relationship will be spent in the growth phase. The mentor and mentee are deepening their professional relationship, specifying goals, and working to achieve them. The focus during this time is on progress.

- Throughout this process, the mentor continues to offer developmental opportunities, activities, constructive feedback, and guidance. The key indicators of this phase are:
- Making steady progress on set goals by undertaking new challenges and tasks together
- Continuing to build trust and rapport
- Demonstrating a commitment to learning and personal growth
- Regularly meeting to discuss progress and goals, as well as challenges and obstacles
- Transferring knowledge and skills from mentor to mentee

The growth phase is typically the longest and most productive stage of a mentoring relationship. It is also where the most value is often derived. In this phase, activities may include:

- Shadow the mentor (attending meetings or presentations) to gain exposure and understanding of a higher level within the organization or industry as a whole
- Identify stretch assignments or projects the mentee can pursue to develop a particular skill
- Solve a particular challenge inhibiting the mentee's progress

This stage requires transparency and humility from the mentee. Similarly, the mentor gives empathy, active listening, and clear feedback.

Phase 4: Completion and Closure

The final stage of mentorship is the completion phase. At some point in your mentoring relationship, you will have hopefully achieved your initial goals and subsequent ones that evolved. The meeting schedule may change, and the conversations certainly will.

One decision is fairly simple. Let your mentor know you have more to learn from them, share the new goals you want to achieve, and request if they will continue the mentoring relationship.

The second option is a little more difficult. You realize it is time to make a transition to a new mentor. You need to let your mentor know you believe you are ready to transition and why. The mentor will want to help their mentee with the transition. They may want to discuss what you are looking for in your next Mentor and make suggestions – potentially an introduction. They may have additional information for you to familiarize yourself with before taking the steps to find your next mentor.

The key indicators of this stage are:

- Achieving the goals set out at the beginning of the mentorship
- Ending on good terms, with both mentor and mentee feeling satisfied with the experience
- Continue progressing and creating new goals
- Sharing of skills and knowledge they've learned to other colleagues or subordinates

It is important for both mentor and mentee to feel a sense of closure at the end of mentorship. Whether this is achieved through celebrating successes or having a sit-down debriefing, both parties should feel like they have gained something from the experience and are ready to move on.

The mentee should ensure they thank the mentor and inform him or her how they appreciate the time spent.

Mentoring relationships hold incredible benefits for both the mentor and mentee. Remember mentorships are like any relationship; they require time, effort, and careful planning to be successful. The right mindset which recognizes the mentoring life cycle recognizes this relationship can make a positive and lasting impact on both the mentor and mentee's life.

TRANSITIONING THE MENTORING RELATIONSHIP: CHECKLIST FOR MENTORS

ENDING THE MENTORING PARTNERSHIP ON GOOD TERMS IS important to ensure the mentor and mentee transition from a mentoring relationship to a strong collegial relationship. To transition as smooth as possible, I recommend mentors use this checklist to help prepare for the final mentoring session.

Mentee: Mentor:

Date of final session:

Task #	Date of Completion	Task
1.		Ensure the mentee is aware of when the final meeting will occur well before it does (introduce the topic around the third to last session).
2.		Approximately one month before conclusion of the mentoring relationship, reflect upon what your mentee has accomplished and what you have gained as a mentor.
3.		Complete evaluation activities (below).
4.		Complete the final meeting reflection and evaluation template prior to the final meeting.

5.		Complete the mentoring program evaluation form and submit it to the mentor program coordinator*, if applicable. *Often used with formal mentoring programs at large organizations or companies.*
6.		Meet with your mentee and discuss responses from the final meeting reflection and evaluation form: • Review the mentee's development plan and goals to measure progress and determine whether you should engage in any subsequent follow-on developmental activities post mentoring relationship. • • Celebrate your mentoring successes and the goals the mentee has achieved. • • Discuss relationship transition with mentee.

https://www.surgeons.org/-/media/Project/RACS/surgeons-org/files/mentoring/racs-41-checklist-for-mentors.pdf

CONCLUSION

I AM HOPEFUL YOU ARE AS EXCITED ABOUT THE NEW, MONumental mentorship journey that awaits you, particularly since I am ever so thrilled for you. Together, we have discussed mentoring principles, processes and practices for your immediate application, so you may expeditiously launch your mentorship journey, or "level up" by leaping along throughout your mentorship journey!

Once again, I want to emphasize how extremely powerful mentorships can be because they connect diverse people, at various levels in their careers, and afford them the support needed to soar to their highest of heights. By now, you know a mentor is someone who can share ideas with you and offer a safe space to turn to for advice. Furthermore, mentors and mentees work together closely as mentors guide, advise, and assist their mentees in achieving successful career goals while navigating through professional challenges.

At this time, I would like to summarize our rich mentoring moments shared via *Mastering Mentoring to Your Vantage Point*. We began by recognizing the amazing opportunity to establish and master a mentoring relationship to aid achievement of your defined goals and desires. We then discussed the eight mentoring models: One-On-One Mentoring, Peer Mentoring, Group Mentoring, Situational Mentoring,

Reverse Mentoring, Speed (or Flash) Mentoring, Team Mentoring and Virtual Mentoring. Also, we identified the essential principles for the mentor, all of which resonate with me because I certainly look to confirm each attribute exists when selecting my mentors.

At present, you should also have a thorough understanding of the comparisons and differences between a mentoring and coaching relationship along with the skills required for mentoring and coaching to be effective. Embracing the value of mentoring will prove to be critical to your success – and the success of your company. It is important to recognize mentoring as a sanctioned investment and not an expense or waste of time. Moreover, understanding how we learn and listen, as well as how others learn and listen, are critical skills for all successful relationships.

Next, we discussed the needed framework from which a strong mentoring relationship should be formed and ultimately mature. Knowing the roles and responsibilities of the mentor and mentee adds such clarity and ensures the boundaries of the mentoring partnership are clearly understood. Since there is no singular method of selecting a mentor, you were reminded to invest the required time to research, interview and select the best mentor to assist you with achieving your goals. Also, on a recurring basis, I recommend revisiting and reassessing your mentoring relationship to ensure they align with your objectives.

Lastly, we concluded learning more about how to politely and respectfully transition the mentor-mentee relationship through the mentoring life cycle.

In closing, I am confident *Mastering Mentoring to Your Vantage Point* will remain a relevant and relatable mentoring workbook; a resource of your choosing to chart your mentoring trajectory today, while preparing to meet your career opportunities of tomorrow. Remember, knowledge is only powerful when applied. So, it is truly essential you process the information shared, and proceed by leveraging all you learned while reading this book.

If you find you are in need of additional information on mentoring, or are interested in a mentoring session with me, I would be delighted to continue to work with you by offering a one-on-one mentoring session. To learn more, please take my advice and first initiate contact by visiting my website **somervilleconsultinggroup.com** to complete a profile and request a mentoring session with me today. I look forward to forming and strengthening our mentoring partnership.

With that said, today, and in the many years to come, may you continue to enjoy your mentorship journey, as much as I have over the decades of being blessed with magnificent mentoring relationships? Remember, I am cheering for you always. Congratulations!